READING REVELATION NONVIOLENTLY

Matthew Curtis Fleischer

Epic Octavius the Triumphant, LLC
Oklahoma City, OK

Published by Epic Octavius the Triumphant, LLC
Oklahoma City, OK

First Edition 2021

ISBN 978-0-9994306-5-1 (paperback)

Printed in the United States of America

Italics in Scripture quotations reflect the author's added emphasis.

Line editing by Christinah Mulder.
Copy editing by Susan Dimmock.
Cover illustration by Anna Hryshchenko.
Cover design by Christian Fuenfhausen.

www.MatthewCurtisFleischer.com

CONTENTS

PREFACE

For the first twenty-five years of my adult life, I shunned the book of Revelation. I didn't understand it, couldn't reconcile it with the Gospels, and despised the violence I thought it glorified and promoted. Recently, however, I've come to appreciate—even love—John's complex, visionary letter.

The book you are now reading, which is an extended excerpt from *Jesus the Pacifist: A Concise Guide to His Radical Nonviolence*, contains the analysis that changed my perspective. If you suffer from the same consternation I once did, my prayer is that the ideas and insights contained herein will do for you what they did for me—open your eyes to the beauty and hope of Revelation, including its profoundly antiviolence message.

Given that this manuscript has been extracted from a larger book, some context is required. For starters, this book is premised on the fact that Jesus is our moral standard. As I discuss at length in *The Old Testament Case for Nonviolence*, the Bible indicates on every level that we are to *obey* Jesus—not Moses or the God of the Old Testament.[1] Likewise, it declares that we are to *mimic* Jesus, not the ancient Israelites, Yahweh, or the God of the end times. Jesus, and Jesus alone, is our ethical ideal, our moral compass, the perfect example of how to do God's will on earth. Everything and everyone in the Bible declares it. Consequently, our analysis of Revelation will focus (primarily, but not exclusively) on Jesus's actions, not God's or that of his angels.

This book also takes Jesus's pre-Revelation pacifism for granted. It assumes you've read the other chapters in *Jesus the Pacifist* and agree that everything about him during his first trip to earth—his actions, teachings, commands, kingship, and death—advocated nonviolence.

Lastly, when I refer to *violence*, I mean the use of (unwelcome) physical force against a person or their property. In other words, I mean it in the relatively narrow, traditional sense, not in the broader, more modern sense of any action that causes any type of physical or nonphysical (verbal, psychological, spiritual, structural, cultural, etc.) harm. Actions that cause the latter types of harm are often as destructive as those that cause physical harm, but they are not our concern here. We are talking about direct physical actions like vandalism, theft, assault, kidnapping, rape, killing, war, and similar tangible acts of coercion, rather than things like insults, income disparities, greed, or racism, which alone are relatively indirect and nonphysical.

---

[1] See Chapter 9, which makes this point from both a historical and theological perspective, backed up by a plethora of Scripture references.

INTRODUCTION

The book of Revelation is infamously violent, easily the most violent book in the New Testament and arguably the most violent book in the entire Bible. Within its pages, people are subjected to plagues and earthquakes, made to drink blood, inflicted with festering sores, poisoned by polluted water, tortured by mutant locusts, tormented with burning sulfur, burned alive, starved to death, dashed to pieces like pottery, crushed by collapsing buildings, flattened by hundred-pound hailstones, gored by wild beasts, eaten by birds, and forced to kill each other. Even children are struck dead. If it was a movie, Revelation would be a horror film.

Most troubling of all, much of the book's violence is attributed—often indirectly, but occasionally directly—to God or Jesus. No wonder Nietzsche described it as "the most rabid outburst of vindictiveness in all recorded history"[1] and Martin Luther claimed he could "in no way detect that the Holy Spirit produced it."[2]

Not helping the situation, Revelation is notoriously difficult to interpret. Throughout Christian history, theologians of all persuasions have acknowledged its complexities and struggled to make sense of its strange, obscure, and elaborate imagery. Many Christians and non-Christians alike view it as the most puzzling part of the most puzzling book ever compiled. Respected intellectuals have called it everything from "a curious record of the visions of a drug addict"[3] to "a book of riddles that requires a revelation to explain."[4]

These two traits—Revelation's seemingly God-sanctioned carnage and its interpretive impenetrability—combine to create a dangerous text. Indeed, throughout history, few pieces of literature have been read with such disastrous results. Christians themselves have frequently weaponized the book, citing it to justify horrendous acts of violence against believers and non-believers alike.[5]

At a minimum, for most Christians, Revelation is the trump card that disproves Christian pacifism and demonstrates the salvific, redemptive nature of violence. It's what ultimately confirms their belief that nonviolence is generally a good thing but not always obligatory, not even for Jesus, and that ultimately only violence can defeat evil.

In a sense, it's hard to blame them. On its face, Revelation does seem to negate the pacifistic Jesus of the Gospels. Instead of continuing to depict a Savior who conquers evil through self-sacrificial love (à la the cross), it appears to portray a Savior who must eventually use violence to finish the job by fighting a "war to end all wars."

Nonetheless, as we are about to see, it is possible to make sense of the book of Revelation, and to do so in a way that confirms Jesus's pacifism and reiterates the nonviolent ethics he taught. In fact, when read within its proper framework, it's a beautifully subversive, deeply antiviolence book.

Granted, Revelation's complexity—with its comingling of genres, its ubiquitous and arcane symbolism, its intertextual nature, and its hodgepodge of worldly and otherworldly phenomena—leaves the door open to a plethora of interpretations. But that doesn't mean all such interpretations are equal. They aren't. Some are demonstrably more reasonable than others, while a not-insignificant number lend credence to G. K. Chesterton's quip that although Revelation's author "saw many strange monsters in his vision, he saw no creature so wild as one of his own commentators."[6]

As with most difficult biblical passages, Revelation forces its reader to make big, important interpretive choices. It presents enough textual proof to support many mutually exclusive readings and makes the reader choose among them. In our case, Revelation can be read violently or nonviolently. Should you desire it, its pages contain enough evidence to support a violent reading. But if you see the wisdom in a nonviolent reading, its pages contain just as much (and, I believe, more) evidence to support that as well.

Regrettably, the nonviolent reading is less popular because it requires two ingredients not possessed by everyone: First, the reader must be open to reading it nonviolently. I can't offer much help here. If you're not willing to even consider a nonviolent reading, and many people aren't, then nothing I can say will suffice.

Second, the reader must willingly put forth the work necessary to read Revelation in context. You will not encounter the nonviolent interpretation via a surface level, literalistic analysis. To see Revelation's antiviolence message, you must go deeper. You must expend the effort to understand its biblical, literary, and historical contexts.

That's what Part I of this book is about. In it, we will explore three key pieces of context. Then, in Part II, we will examine Revelation's violence in light of that context and the antiviolence symbols and themes arising from it.

---

[1] Friedrich Nietzsche, *The Birth of Tragedy and the Genealogy of Morals*, trans. Francis Golffing (Garden City, NY: Doubleday, 1956 [1887]), 185.

[2] Michael J. Gorman, *Reading Revelation Responsibly: Uncivil Worship and Witness Following the Lamb Into the New Creation* (Eugene, OR: Cascade Books, 2011), 1.

[3] George Bernard Shaw, as quoted in Preston Sprinkle's *Fight: A Christian Case for Non-Violence* (David C. Cook, 2013), 2589, Kindle.

[4] Thomas Paine, as quoted in Michael J. Gorman's *Reading Revelation Responsibly: Uncivil Worship and Witness Following the Lamb Into the New Creation* (Cascade Books, 2011), 198, Kindle.

[5] For example, according to Wes Howard-Brook and Anthony Gwyther, Revelation "has been used and abused to support a wide variety of social movements, from the modern-day Branch Davidians incinerated at Waco and the Heaven's Gate community … to the second-century Montanists and the thirteenth-century Apostolic Brethren." They also claim that its "underlying schema of history inspired, consciously or unconsciously, Hitler's notion

of the Third Reich and Karl Marx's dream of the revolution of the proletariat." See *Unveiling Empire: Reading Revelation Then and Now* (Orbis Books, 1999), 607, Kindle.

[6] G. K. Chesterton, *Orthodoxy*, Centennial Edition (Nashville: Sam Torode Book Arts, 2009), 13.

PART I
SETTING THE SCENE

CHAPTER 1
THE APOCALYPTIC GENRE

The first step to properly interpreting any writing is identifying and understanding its literary genre. We need to know whether we are reading poetry, journalism, science fiction, or academic history because we interpret them differently. For instance, no one reads the poetic Psalms the same way they read Paul's rhetorical argumentation in his letter to the Romans, and neither of them are read in the same manner as the gospel narratives. To do so, to approach them with the same expectations and perspectives, would be foolish.

The same is true for Revelation, but doubly so. Most misinterpretations of it, particularly those that turn it into a dangerous text, are rooted in a fundamental misunderstanding of its literary form and purpose.

Unfortunately, Revelation doesn't fit neatly into a single genre. It is a hybrid of multiple literary forms, including letter, apocalypse, prophecy, and liturgy. Nonetheless, it does clearly have a dominant genre: apocalypse. It begins by proclaiming itself to be "The revelation of Jesus Christ," wherein "revelation" is the English form of the Greek word *apokalypsis*.[1] Therefore, to properly interpret Revelation, we need to understand a bit about apocalyptic writing as it was used by the biblical writers and throughout the ancient Near East.

When most people today hear the word *apocalypse*, they think of a world-ending cataclysmic event, usually involving violent natural disasters like earthquakes, tsunamis, or asteroid showers. But in Greek, the word means "an unveiling." It means to reveal, to uncover, to unmask. Biblical apocalyptic writing is, as N.T. Wright describes, "the sudden unveiling of a previously hidden truth."[2] The author has been allowed to see things others haven't, to see aspects of reality that aren't readily apparent, and he desires to pass them on. This is the purpose of Revelation. Wright explains:

> John, its author ... is picking up a way of writing well known in the Jewish world of the time. This way of writing was designed to correspond to, and make available, the visions and 'revelations' seen by holy, prayerful people who were wrestling with the question of the divine purpose. Like the theatre audience, they and the rest of God's people felt themselves in the dark. As they studied their ancient scriptures and said their prayers, they believed that the music was building up to something, but nobody was quite sure what. But then, like someone all by themselves in the theatre for the first performance, the 'seer'—the word reflects the reality, 'one who sees' something that other people do not—finds that the curtain is suddenly pulled up. Suddenly the 'seer' is witnessing a scene, is in fact invited to be part of a scene, within God's ongoing drama.[3]

Similarly, apocalyptic writing is prophetic, but not in the modern sense of the word. It is prophetic in the biblical sense, which is less about predicting the future and more about explaining the present, less about foretelling future reality and more about truthfully describing current reality. It unmasks what is really going on, how the fallen world really works—not merely how it will be at some future point. Prophecy, in the biblical tradition, intends to provide insight into today as much as foresight about tomorrow. It is as much about the human historical experience here and now as it is about history written in advance.

Combining these two aspects of Revelation—the apocalyptic (in the Greek sense) and the prophetic (in the biblical sense)—allows us to understand the book as the unveiling of present reality from God's perspective. It is, in other words, the unveiling of true reality. Hence the book opens by proclaiming itself to be a recording of what God has revealed to its author, John, who in Chapter 4 of

Revelation describes how he was taken up to God's throne room to view the unfolding of everything else described in its remaining eighteen chapters.[4]

Of course, Revelation has something to say about the future. There is a predictive aspect to it. But it is not, contrary to popular evangelical opinion, a codebook of end-time events just waiting to be properly deciphered.

To begin with, its predictions aren't hidden. Apocalyptic writing in the biblical tradition employs symbolism to *uncover* how reality works, not *encode* future events. It intends to *reveal*, not *conceal*. Revelation's predictions need not be hidden because they aren't about specific details or events. Instead, they are about general, big-picture consequences and happenings. Revelation predicts things like (1) what life on earth will continue to be like as long as humans persist in embodying Satan's kingdom instead of God's (i.e., as long as they continue living violently instead of lovingly),[5] and (2) God's eventual, total, and final defeat of evil and injustice and the complete reestablishment of his kingdom on earth.

The wildly creative, otherworldly, fantasy-laden, over-the-top characters and scenes Revelation employs to make such broad prophecies were not intended to provide a historically accurate chronicling of actual events that must occur before such things will come to pass, let alone supply a realistic description of how each will literally unfold. Rather, they were, in keeping with the apocalyptic genre and the oral culture of the day, designed for dramatic appeal, memorability, and symbolic communication. Revelation is not a puzzle to be solved by identifying which symbols represent which historical figures and events, but "a visionary theological and poetic representation of the spiritual environment within which the church perennially finds itself living and struggling," to borrow Richard Hays' description.[6]

Revelation's use of symbolism cannot be overemphasized. Apocalyptic literature communicates almost entirely, if not entirely, through symbolism. It speaks through pictures, not logic. It appeals to the imagination, not rational deduction. It aims to influence its hearers by providing them with an imaginative experience, not by filling them full of facts. It employs graphic, emotionally charged symbols in order to awake and arouse, not to impart academically accurate data. It is theatrical, not scientific.

Here's the most important thing about symbolism, both in general and in Revelation: By definition, it isn't meant to be interpreted literally. Something is symbolic when it is figurative, representative, illustrative, emblematic, or allegorical. In other words, something is symbolic precisely when and because it is *not* literal. Thus, Revelation employs symbolism precisely so it will *not* be read literally as an imparting of encyclopedic facts about how God will eradicate evil, when the world will end, etc. Jesus himself set the tone for a nonliteral interpretation of Revelation when, during his instructions to its author in the first chapter, he explained that the seven golden lampstands and seven stars were *symbols* for the seven churches and their seven angels.[7]

Symbolism seeks to express the invisible or immaterial through visible representation. Symbols are employed to communicate intangible literal truths, not to depict literal beings or events. As such, Revelation's symbolism is meant to be interpreted truthfully, but not literally. Its word pictures aim to give visible representation to theological truths, not provide a literal depiction of theological characters and events.

For example, Jesus is not literally a lamb. He isn't covered in wool and doesn't walk around on four legs while chewing grass and saying "baaa." But he is vulnerable and nonviolent like a lamb. And he was sacrificially slaughtered like one.

Likewise, the 144,000 virgins with God's name written on their head who are said to have never told a lie aren't literally 144,000 individuals who have tattooed their faces, never had sex, and never been untruthful. It is a symbolic number representing a large number (which derives from 12 x 12 x 1,000, being the number of Israel's tribes squared and then multiplied by Revelation's number of magnitude and power), of God's faithful followers—those who have clung to the truth and not defiled themselves with idolatry, which is often symbolized in the Bible as adultery or sexual promiscuity.

Similarly, Revelation's use of "millennium" and "thousand years" isn't intended to denote a literal period of one thousand calendar years but instead symbolically denotes a long, indefinite time period. At least, that's what it meant to the Jewish people and other biblical writers. When the Psalmist wrote that God owns the cattle on a thousand hills, he wasn't claiming that God's ownership of cattle is limited to *only* one thousand hills.[8] And when he declared that one day in God's courts is better than a thousand elsewhere, he wasn't claiming that 1,001 days elsewhere would be better than one day in God's courts.[9]

In fact, if we interpret all of Revelation's symbols literally, the book would end in Chapter 6. There, we see described the sun turning black, the moon turning blood red, the stars falling to earth, the heavens receding like a scroll being rolled up, and every mountain and island being dislodged.[10] If all of that literally occurred, life on earth would cease to exist. But the story, along with human life, goes on. The stars even magically reappear in the sky in Chapters 8 and 12, only to be partially destroyed again each time.[11] As this single example demonstrates, applying a literal lens to all of Revelation's visionary imagery produces logical absurdities and contradictions.

Selective literal interpretations won't do either. In many ways, they are worse. They betray the interpreter's self-interested agenda, revealing his presuppositions through what he does and doesn't want to be literal. Here's what Brian Zahnd says on the subject:

If some people admit that the lamb with seven horns and seven eyes is obviously symbolic but insist that Jesus riding a flying white horse is literal, they're going to have to explain their system of interpretation. Or if they claim that Jesus is going to wage a literal war upon his return but the sword depicted as proceeding from his mouth is symbolic, again they're going to have to justify the logic of their system.[12]

In one of his recorded sermons, Pastor Bill Johnson highlighted the hypocrisy of interpreting some of Revelation's symbols literally but not others.[13] During a discussion of the passage in Revelation 20 that describes the dragon being bound with chains and cast into a bottomless pit for a thousand years, he had the following conversation with his audience, who at the time believed in a literal millennium:

Bill: The Dragon, literal or figurative? Is it a real dragon?

Audience: Figurative.

Bill: The chains, literal or figurative? Is it actual chains?

Audience: Figurative.

Bill: The bottomless pit, literal or figurative?

Audience: Figurative.

Bill: The millennium, literal or figurative?

Audience: (stunned silence)

We could go on, but you get the point. "The only way to consistently interpret the book of Revelation," Zahnd concludes, "is to acknowledge that *everything* is communicated by symbol."[14] To interpret Revelation's visionary imagery literally is to misinterpret it. Doing so not only violates the genre but causes one logical problem after another. To interpret it correctly, we must acknowledge its symbolic nature and fix our eyes on the literal truths it communicates, not treat it as a codebook of literal end-time characters, events, and timelines.

John's original audience would have intuitively understood all of this. While many of its symbols are mysterious to us two thousand years after its writing, they would have been familiar to those who shared John's cultural, political, historical, and religious context. As Hays puts it, they "would have read such symbolism 'as fluently as any modern reader of the daily papers reads the conventional symbols of a political cartoon.'"[15] To be more precise, they would have noticed and understood its symbolism as effortlessly as "American readers of a political cartoon featuring an elephant and a donkey immediately know that the elephant symbolizes the Republican party and that the donkey symbolizes the Democrats."[16]

We must never forget that Revelation was written by a first-century author to a first-century audience to address first-century problems using first-century literary devices and images.[17]

---

[1] Rev. 1:1.

[2] N. T. Wright, *Revelation for Everyone* (Westminster John Knox Press, 2011), 146, Kindle.

[3] Ibid.

[4] Rev. 1:1-2, 10-11; 4:1-2.

[5] Or as Zack Hunt describes it, "The [biblical] prophets weren't fortune-tellers. They were warning the people of God about what would happen in the future if they did or didn't act a certain way in the present. Which is why biblical prophecy is about the present as much as or more than it is about the future." In other words, "Revelation isn't a road map to the future. It's a model for how to live in the present.... This is, after all, why John's apocalypse begins with letters to churches in the present, with instructions on how to live in the here and now." See *Unraptured: How End Times Theology Gets it Wrong* (Herald Press, 2019), 2114 and 2320, Kindle.

[6] Richard Hays, *The Moral Vision of the New Testament: Community, Cross, New Creation; A Contemporary Introduction to New Testament Ethics* (HarperOne, 2013), 4872, Kindle.

[7] Rev. 1:20.

[8] Ps. 50:10.

[9] Ps. 84:10.

[10] Rev. 6:12-14.

[11] Rev. 8:12; 12:4.

[12] Brian Zahnd, *Sinners in the Hands of a Loving God: The Scandalous Truth of the Very Good News* (WaterBrook, 2017), 2063, Kindle.

[13] Bill Johnson, "Mission Possible," CD. 15:30 minute mark to 17:05 minute mark.

[14] Zahnd, *Sinners in the Hands of a Loving God*, 2063.

[15] Hays, *The Moral Vision of the New Testament*, 4848 (citing G. B. Caird 1956, *Principalities and Powers*, Oxford: Clarendon, 6).

[16] Ibid., 4849.

[17] This is not my description but a paraphrase of a point Gorman made in *Reading Revelation Responsibly*. See Kindle location 1703.

CHAPTER 2
THE BIBLE'S WARFARE WORLDVIEW

The second piece of context necessary to properly interpret the violence in Revelation is the Bible's warfare worldview.

The Bible frames reality in terms of a great war between God and Satan, between good and evil, between the kingdom of light and the kingdom of darkness. According to the Bible, the story of the universe is the story of God's creation, Satan's subsequent invasion, and God's gradual restoration of his kingdom, on earth as it is in heaven. Everything in the Bible occurs in this context, from Satan's role in the Garden of Eden to God's final destruction of the beast in Revelation.[1] "There is no neutral ground in the universe," wrote C. S. Lewis. "Every square inch, every split second, is claimed by God and counterclaimed by Satan."[2]

Throughout both Testaments, the Bible uses words like "kingdom," "rule," "dominion," and "sovereignty" to describe what God was doing—through Israel, the prophets, Jesus, the apostles, and the early church. Even the titles that frequently preface the names of God and Jesus are loaded with earthly kingdom implications. The Bible regularly refers to God as "God of gods," "Lord of lords," and "Lord of heaven and earth,"[3] while it similarly calls Jesus "Lord of lords and King of kings."[4]

The Bible establishes Satan as God's adversary, calling him things like "the enemy," "the evil one," and "the prince of demons."[5] And it doesn't merely refer to Satan as *an* enemy or *an* evil one, but as *the* enemy and *the* evil one. Satan and God are so antithetical they are often symbolically contrasted as darkness versus light,[6] with Paul labeling Satan "the dominion of darkness" (Col. 1:13).

The Bible also frequently gives Satan credit for ruling the world, identifying him as "the prince of this world," "the god of this age," and "the ruler of the kingdom of the air."[7] According to 1 John 5:19, "the whole world is under the control of the evil one." And when Satan promised to give Jesus all the kingdoms of the world if he disobeyed God, Jesus didn't question the evil one's possession of them.[8] Furthermore, as we will explore in the next chapter, Satan's power over all nations and people is a prevalent theme throughout the book of Revelation.[9] As Greg Boyd concludes, "while Jesus and his followers of course believed that God was the *ultimate* Lord over creation, it is apparent that Jesus viewed Satan as the *functional* ruler over the earth at the present time."[10]

Throughout the Bible, Satan is engaged in constant conflict with God's kingdom. He has been attempting to thwart it since the beginning.[11] He is "the enemy of everything that is right," "full of all kinds of deceit and trickery," and constantly "perverting the right ways of the Lord" (Acts 13:10). He deceives the nations and leads the entire world astray.[12] "He is a liar" who "masquerades as an angel of light" (John 8:44; 2 Cor. 11:14). He sows strife and incites people to disobey God.[13] He uses sinful desires to enslave us and wage war against our souls and bodies.[14] He blocks believers' attempts to spread the gospel, and he prevents individuals from hearing and understanding God's Word.[15] He "prowls around like a roaring lion looking for someone to devour" (1 Pet. 5:8). Occasionally, he even competes directly against God for the obedience of human beings, including Jesus.[16] "In the Bible," writes Richard Beck, "Satan and the Devil are interchangeable names for the personification of all that is adversarial to the kingdom and people of God, the personified Enemy of God."[17]

Jesus's Nemesis

While Jesus was on earth, he was constantly battling Satan. As soon as Jesus was born, Satan tried to kill him,[18] and immediately after God pronounced Jesus to be the Messiah, Satan engaged him in the wilderness, tempting him with all the kingdoms of the world in exchange for worship.[19] From that day forward, Jesus spent much of his remaining time on earth combating Satan's handiwork by healing those who were under his power, sometimes by curing diseases and other times by casting out demons.[20] Eventually, Satan's evil forces orchestrated Jesus's crucifixion, prompting Judas to betray him.[21] No wonder Jesus called Satan a "murderer from the beginning," the "father of lies," and a "stumbling block to me" (John 8:43-44; Matt. 16:23). As Dietrich Bonhoeffer concluded, "the whole of his life was one long conflict with the devil."[22]

Evidence of this conflict is everywhere in the Gospels. Consider how Jesus's healings and exorcisms are described. They are portrayed as skirmishes in the ongoing war between God's kingdom and Satan's. Through these healings, Jesus was reclaiming captured territory and people. He was restoring the lives that Satan had destroyed, setting people free from the devil's anti-human grip. For "if it is by the Spirit of God that I drive out demons," proclaimed Jesus, "then the kingdom of God has come upon you" (Matt. 12:28). Similarly, when John the Baptist asked Jesus whether he was the promised Messiah, Jesus justified his affirmative claim by pointing to his restorative miracles: "The blind receive sight, the lame walk, those who have leprosy are cleansed, the deaf hear, the dead are raised, and the good news is proclaimed to the poor" (Matt. 11:5).

Jesus came to earth to defeat Satan's rule and set us free from bondage. He came to "destroy the devil's work," condemn him, drive him out, and break his power, including his power in death.[23] He came to replace Satan's kingdom of evil, death, oppression, bloodshed, hatred, vengeance, sickness, poverty, suffering, darkness, temptation, deception, falsehood, and division with God's kingdom of peace, truth, light, joy, beauty, freedom, health, abundance, relationship, brotherhood, and unity. He came to set creation free, to liberate it from enslavement to sin and all of sin's negative effects—psychological, physical, spiritual, social, and environmental.[24] He came to overthrow the tyranny of the devil and render evil powerless, to conquer injustice and restore justice, to eradicate death and give life.

Simply put, Jesus came to earth to advance God's kingdom over and against Satan's. This was the central theme, the primary mission, of his entire life and ministry. He focused all his efforts on turning the kingdom of the world into the kingdom of God. It is why he lived and died and rose again.

Jesus himself declared this to be his purpose: "I must proclaim the good news of the kingdom of God to the other towns also, because that is why I was sent" (Luke 4:43). To proclaim the arrival of God's kingdom was to declare war on Satan's kingdom, including earthly kingdoms that operate through his evil means of violence and power. Labeling this proclamation the "gospel" and "good news" would have made this evident to Jesus's audience, as Frank Viola explains:

> In the first century, the words "gospel" and "evangelize" referred to heralding the good news that a new emperor had been installed in the Roman Empire. Heralds would go out to proclaim the good news, informing people that a new era of peace, salvation, and blessing had begun.... The apostles used this same language to describe the preaching of the gospel of Jesus Christ. The gospel that the apostles preached was the announcement—the heralding—that Jesus of Nazareth had become this world's true Emperor (Lord), launching a new era of peace, salvation, and blessing, and because of it, everything has changed.[25]

Jesus's entire message was unmistakably kingdom-centered. He didn't just preach about God, the good news, or the gospel. He preached about the *kingdom* of God (or as Matthew calls it, the kingdom of heaven),[26] the good news of the *kingdom* of God, and the gospel of the *kingdom*.[27] His arrival marked a fundamental change in the biblical message, from the law and the prophets to the "good news of the kingdom of God" (Luke 16:16).[28] His earliest public announcement was "Repent, for the kingdom of heaven has come near" (Matt. 4:17).

Jesus spoke more about the kingdom of God than about any other topic. He spent his entire ministry talking about it—what it is like, how to enter it, who is and isn't there, who is the greatest in it, how it differs from worldly kingdoms, how it will triumph over all other earthly kingdoms, etc.[29] Even after he was crucified, died, and rose from the grave, he immediately resumed talking about the kingdom of God.[30]

Of course, Jesus also spoke about his dying for our sins, giving us eternal life, and other aspects of personal salvation, but those things, while important, were not his primary message. They were subparts of a larger, more central theme that tied them—and everything else in Scripture—together: the advancement of God's kingdom on earth as it is in heaven.

But don't take my word for it. Open your Bible and check it out. Once you know to look for it, you'll find kingdom talk everywhere. It permeates the Gospels. The kingdom of God is nothing less than the purpose and goal of human history.

The Victory of the Cross

Jesus's conflict with Satan reached its climax on the cross. To the world, it looked—and still looks—like Satan won. In a world that values control and survival above all else, being tortured to death as a seemingly helpless outcast was a clear and total defeat. In fact, it was about as painful and humiliating of a defeat as possible.

But Christianity proclaims this climatic moment a victory. "And having disarmed the powers and authorities, [Jesus] made a public spectacle of them, triumphing over them by the cross" (Col. 2:15). Jesus "shared in their humanity so that by his death he might break the power of him who holds the power of death—that is, the devil—and free those who all their lives were held in slavery by their fear of death" (Heb. 2:14-15). "The sting of death is sin, and the power of sin is the law. But thanks be to God! He gives us the victory through our Lord Jesus Christ" (1 Cor. 15:56-57). Referring to his own impending death, Jesus said, "Now is the time for judgment on this world; now the prince of this world will be driven out" (John 12:31). After all, "The reason the Son of God appeared was to destroy the devil's work" (1 John 3:8).

However paradoxical it may seem, the entire New Testament declares Jesus's crucifixion a victory over Satan and his kingdom. "Every major strand of the New Testament," writes John Howard Yoder, "each in its own way, interprets the acceptance by Jesus of the violence of the cross as the means, necessary and sufficient, of God's victory over the rebellious powers."[31] And as Lee C. Camp observes, "the New Testament closes with this very assertion: that it is the slaughtered Lamb who is worshiped as the victorious one, triumphing over the enemies of God."[32] Jesus accomplished many other things on the cross,[33] but he also, and not least of all, conquered his archenemy, including that enemy's most powerful weapon—death.[34]

Thus, the cross isn't a barrier to, prerequisite for, or consequence of Jesus's victory. It is the victory itself. It is the triumph of good over evil. In other words, it isn't just Jesus who defeated Satan. It is the *crucified* Jesus. He is "now crowned with glory and honor *because* he suffered death" (Heb. 2:9).

Of course, the resurrection is important too. Essential, in fact. But it wasn't the victory; the cross was.[35] The cross was the victory because it is where Jesus's lifetime of perfect love reached its completion and ultimate expression. It is where he endured the worst evil could do to him without straying from the way of love. Jesus triumphed over evil not by rising from the dead but by always loving (and remaining nonviolent), even unto death. The resurrection simply proved it. Strictly speaking, the cross was the victory and the resurrection was the vindication of (and reward for) that victory.

To describe the victory in slightly different terms, by his death and resurrection Jesus became, and remains, king on earth. Because of this victory, he is now in charge. "He is the head over every power and authority" (Col. 2:10). God "raised Christ from the dead and seated him at his right hand in the heavenly realms, far above all rule and authority, power and dominion, and every name that is invoked, not only in the present age but also in the one to come" (Eph. 1:20-21). Jesus is now "at God's right hand—with angels, authorities and powers in submission to him" (1 Pet. 3:22). "All authority in heaven and on earth has been given to me," declared the risen Jesus (Matt. 28:18). Even according to the book of Revelation, Jesus is already—prior to his second coming— "the ruler of the kings of the earth" (Rev. 1:5).[36] The entire New Testament declares it.

N. T. Wright calls this fact "the forgotten story of the gospels."[37] He claims we have almost entirely forgotten that "devastating and challenging message," which "the past two hundred years of European and American culture have been desperately trying to stifle."[38] He's got a point. When is the last time you heard a sermon on Jesus's earthly kingship or the Kingdom of God? Nevertheless, "the story of Jesus is the story of how Israel's God became king on earth," and "the whole point of the gospels" is to tell that story.[39] Indeed, "once you lose the kingdom-theme, which is central to the gospels," Wright adds, "everything else becomes reinterpreted in ways that radically distort" their messages.[40] "The gospels are not about 'how Jesus turned out to be God.' They are about *how God became king on earth as in heaven.*"[41]

That being said, Jesus's victory isn't yet complete. He has initiated his earthly kingship, but he isn't yet earth's sole ruler. Satan still reigns, in part. Nonetheless, Jesus has won a pivotal battle. His life, death, and resurrection set in motion the beginning of the end of Satan's kingdom. Like D-Day in WWII, he didn't end the war between God and Satan but he did strike the decisive blow that determined who will eventually and inevitably win it. Total victory is assured but not yet realized. Sin, death, and evil itself have been conquered, but not yet eradicated.

In this sense, God's kingdom is already, but not yet. It is already here, but not yet fully here. It is present, yet future, which is why Jesus often referred to God's kingdom in the present *and* future tense.[42]

Eventually, Jesus will finish the job. He will bring the future into fulfillment. He will return to earth to annihilate all remaining evil power and finalize God's total and eternal reign.[43] He will complete what he started in the Gospels: the re-establishment of God's kingdom on earth as it is in heaven. If his death and resurrection was D-Day, his second coming will be V-Day, the final victory that will end all conflict, pain, suffering, and death.[44] The whole Bible testifies to this truth, and even the devil knows it.[45]

Analogizing the Christian as Soldier

This warfare worldview explains why Jesus and the New Testament writers employ so many military metaphors. Our Christian purpose is located within this ongoing battle. God has tasked us with continuing the fight, with taking back territory for his kingdom, with spreading his sovereign rule and dominion on earth as it is in heaven. "Enemy-occupied territory—that is what this world is," wrote C.S. Lewis.

"Christianity is the story of how the rightful king has landed, you might say landed in disguise, and is calling us to take part in a great campaign of sabotage."[46] "To be a Christian is to be a warrior," concluded Charles H. Spurgeon. "The good soldier of Jesus Christ must not expect to find ease in this world; it is a battlefield."[47]

God's earthly battle against evil rages on and we are an important part of it. To be baptized is to be conscripted into God's army and to join his costly campaign against Satan's violent, destructive, oppressive, exploitative, death-wielding kingdom.

Hence all of the New Testament's soldiering and fighting metaphors. On two occasions, Paul described fellow Christians as "fellow soldiers" (Phil. 2:25; Philem. 1:2). On another, he wrote, "Join with me in suffering, like a good soldier of Christ Jesus. No one serving as a soldier gets entangled in civilian affairs, but rather tries to please his commanding officer" (2 Tim. 2:3-4). Likewise, Peter instructed his readers to "arm yourselves" with a willingness to suffer like Jesus did (1 Pet. 4:1). Paul encouraged Timothy to "keep your head in all situations, endure hardship, do the work of an evangelist, discharge all the duties of your ministry," just as he himself had "fought the good fight," finished the race, and kept the faith (2 Tim. 4:5-7). In what is likely the most famous New Testament military metaphor, Paul instructed Christians to ready themselves for battle with the devil by putting on "the full armor of God," including the "belt of truth," "breastplate of righteousness," boots of readiness, "shield of faith," "helmet of salvation," and "sword of the Spirit, which is the word of God" (Eph. 6:10-17).[48] "As servants of God," he wrote, we equip ourselves "with weapons of righteousness in the right hand and in the left" (2 Cor. 6:4-7). "So let us put aside the deeds of darkness and put on the armor of light" (Rom. 13:12). We must "fight the battle well" and "fight the good fight of the faith ... until the appearing of our Lord Jesus Christ" (1 Tim. 1:18; 6:12-14).

Note that although these passages compare the Christian mission to soldiering, none of them do so in a way that communicates anything positive about soldiering or violence in general. They all praise wholly nonviolent attributes, none of which are unique to soldiering but most of which are best *analogized* in soldiers: complete devotion to a commanding officer, a willingness to sacrifice and suffer for a cause greater than oneself, execution of duty regardless of the cost, self-discipline, endurance, faithfulness, equipping yourself for (spiritual) battle, etc.[49]

In reality, all the New Testament's military metaphors tell Christians to be *like* soldiers in their nonviolent attributes (e.g., their singleness of purpose, their disciplined pursuit of such, and their willingness to suffer and sacrifice to achieve it) but *unlike* soldiers in their violent attributes (e.g., by telling them to wage war with nonviolent weapons like truth, righteousness, preparedness, faith, and salvation instead of with violent weapons like swords, spears, and arrows).

These metaphors encourage Christians to wage war, but to do so only with nonviolent weapons. That's their whole point: fight like typical soldiers, but don't use the same weapons as typical soldiers. For as Paul declared, "though we live in the world, we do not wage war as the world does. The weapons we fight with are not the weapons of the world" (2 Cor. 10:3-4). This is because we fight a different type of enemy: "For our struggle is not against flesh and blood, but against the rulers, against the authorities, against the powers of this dark world and against the spiritual forces of evil in the heavenly realms" (Eph. 6:12).

To state it more directly, the military metaphors don't compare Christians to soldiers in every way. Instead, they compare them in some ways and contrast them in others. That's what metaphors do—they compare *non-identical* things. We must keep the differences intact. We must not lose sight of which military characteristics are being promoted and which aren't. The military metaphors only commend what they actually say they commend, and when we look carefully, we see that none of them commend violence. Instead, they contrast the physical weapons of violence with the spiritual weapons of nonviolence and call Christians to equip themselves with the latter, not the former.

To cite the New Testament's military metaphors as supporting the use of violence contradicts the very point they were employed to make. They employ warfare imagery to promote nonviolence, not violence. "Rightly understood," Hays writes, "these metaphors witness powerfully against violence as an expression of obedience to God in Christ." In them, "the warfare imagery is drafted into the service of the gospel, rather than the reverse."[50] Or as Guy Frank Hershberger warned, "The Christian warfare as described in the New Testament is of such a nature that one cannot use it as an argument for the military warfare of nations without doing great violence to the Scriptures."[51]

Why the Bible Uses Warfare Terminology

Jesus and the New Testament writers employ warfare terminology not to condone violence but to communicate that an urgent, universal conflict of utmost importance is underway, one that God wants us to join him in and one that will require the same commitment, discipline, and self-sacrifice as waging a violent war.

When you need to convey ideas of this magnitude, particularly the seriousness of what's at stake, sports analogies simply won't do. This isn't a game. It is life and death. The fate of creation hangs in the balance.

The violent metaphors, analogies, and parables are also not meant to provide ethical guidance on the proper use of violence. They don't give us our marching orders. They give context to our marching orders. They don't detail our rules of engagement. They give meaning to our rules of engagement. They don't teach us *how* to fight evil. They reaffirm our calling *to* fight evil in the first place.

To determine how God wants us to fight evil, we must look to Jesus's actual ethical instructions. Jesus didn't always speak in analogies, metaphors, and parables. He did make direct propositional statements, and he did issue commands—see the Sermon on the Mount.

When we look to the Sermon on the Mount, and to Jesus's other ethical teachings, we clearly see that he wants us to fight nonviolently. His battle plan is simple: love. That's it. To wage war on evil as Jesus taught and did, we need only to serve others nonviolently. The war we are fighting, the war between God and Satan, is a war between love and unlove, nonviolence and violence.

Revelation and the Warfare Worldview

Here's the point of presenting all this warfare worldview evidence: Revelation takes it to the next level. It is the most explicit, most graphic description of God's ongoing war with Satan in all of Scripture. It is cosmic theater on a grand scale, depicting God engaged in an epic, universal, all-important, very real, life-and-death struggle for sovereignty over the world. The entire book is about how God's kingdom (through Jesus and his followers) has been, is, and will continue taking back territory (and the pain, setbacks, and difficulties associated with such an endeavor) until it conquers all. It is the climax of the clash between good and evil, phrased in terms of the Lamb versus the Beast, angels versus demons, Christians versus earthly empires, and New Jerusalem versus Babylon.

Here is Revelation's main narrative: God's kingdom fights, suffers, and eventually triumphs over Satan's. This, Michael J. Gorman explains, is what apocalyptic writing is all about:

Apocalyptic literature gives expression to apocalyptic theology. At the core of this kind of theology is a *cosmic* dualism, the belief that there are two opposing forces at work in the universe, one for evil (usually Satan and his demons) and one for good (usually God and the angels). This cosmic dualism gets embodied in real-life struggles between good and evil on earth, resulting in a more *historical* dualism of conflict between the children of God or light and the children of Satan or darkness.[52]

But just like all of the other violent imagery in the New Testament, Revelation's imagery is metaphorical and analogical. Yes, it is the great cosmic conflict on steroids, but they are symbolic steroids. Its warfare imagery is not meant to be interpreted literally. It isn't even the main point. It is used illustratively, as a means of making some other, more primary point. More specifically, it employs violent warfare imagery not to condone physical violence or human warfare (or teach us some other ethical lesson about how to properly use violence for good) but to communicate the reality of God's universal war against evil and our soldier-like role in it. We must not let the means of communication—the heavily symbolic and highly dramatic apocalyptic genre—distract us from the message that is truly being communicated.

So yes, Revelation declares that we are engaged in battle. Yes, it is a call to arms and a command to conquer. But it does not call us to a physical battle or to violent action. It calls us to fight a more important war, a spiritual war, and to fight it by remaining faithful to the way of Jesus—not by wielding earthly power. In fact, it commands us to fight evil by *refraining* from violence. It implores us to *resist* the allure of violent warfare. Yes, it uses militaristic language, but it does so in an anti-militaristic way, just like Paul's soldiering metaphors. This will become evident as our analysis proceeds.

By the way, to say that we must interpret Revelation's violent imagery within the context of the Bible's larger warfare worldview is simply to say that we must interpret it within the context of the rest of Scripture. Proper exegesis demands it. As a subset of the Bible, Revelation must be read and understood through the lens of the rest of the Bible, not vice versa. We must filter what it says about God and Jesus through what we already know about them as revealed in the rest of the Canon, particularly the Gospels.

---

[1] For general additional info on how prevalent the theme of spiritual warfare is throughout the entire Bible, see Richard Beck's *Reviving Old Scratch: Demons and the Devil for Doubters and the Disenchanted* (InterVarsity Press, 2015), and for a more specific treatment, see also Chapters 21-24 ("The Principle of Cosmic Conflict") in Greg Boyd's *The Crucifixion of the Warrior God.*

[2] C. S. Lewis, "Christianity and Culture" in *Christian Reflections*, ed. Walter Hover (Grand Rapids: Eerdmans, 1967), 33.

[3] Deut. 10:17; Ps. 136:2-3; Dan. 2:47; Matt. 11:25; Luke 10:21; Acts 17:24. First Timothy 6:15 also refers to God as "the blessed and only Ruler, the King of kings and Lord of lords," and Revelation 15:3 calls him "King of the nations."

[4] Rev. 17:14; 19:11-16. In the Old Testament, "Lord" is often a translation for the Hebrew word *adon*, which means one possessed of absolute control or a master or a ruler of his subjects. In the New Testament, "Lord" is almost universally a translation for the Greek word *kurios*, which means master.

[5] Luke 10:19; Matt. 13:38; 1 John 5:19; John 17:15; Matt. 12:24; Mark 3:22; Luke 11:15.

[6] Eph. 6:11-12; Acts 26:17-18; Col. 1:12-13.

[7] John 12:31; 14:30; 16:11; 2 Cor. 4:4; Eph. 2:2.

[8] Matt. 4:8-10; Luke 4:5-8.

[9] Rev. 12:9, 17; 13:3-4, 7-8, 12, 14-17; 14:8; 17:2; 18:3, 23; 20:3, 7-8.

[10] Gregory A. Boyd, *The Crucifixion of the Warrior God: Interpreting the Old Testament's Violent Portraits of God in Light of the Cross, Volumes 1 & 2* (Fortress Press, 2017), 22579, Kindle.

[11] 1 John 3:8; 2 Cor. 11:3.

[12] Rev. 12:9; 20:3.

[13] Matt. 13:36-43; Acts 5:3; 1 Chron. 21:1; 1 Cor. 7:5; Eph. 2:1-2; 1 John 3:8.

[14] 1 Pet. 2:11; Rom. 6:12; Gal. 4:3-9.

[15] 1 Thess. 2:18; 2 Cor. 12:7; Matt. 13:19; Mark 4:15; Luke 8:12; 2 Cor. 4:4.

[16] See generally Genesis, Job, and Revelation. For his courting of Jesus, see Matt. 4:1-10, Luke 4:5-8, and Mark 8:33.

[17] Richard Beck, *Reviving Old Scratch: Demons and the Devil for Doubters and the Disenchanted* (Fortress Press, 2016), 275, Kindle.

[18] Rev. 12:4; Matt. 2:13-16.

[19] Matt. 3:13-4:11; Luke 3:21-4:13; Mark 1:9-13.

[20] For example, see Mark 1:23-34; 3:9-11; 5:1-42; 7:24-30; Matt. 12:22-28; 15:22-28; Luke 4:31-39; 11:14-20; 13:10-13; Acts 10:37-38.

[21] John 13:2, 27; Luke 22:2-4.

[22] Dietrich Bonhoeffer, *The Cost of Discipleship* (Touchstone, 2012), 1836, Kindle.

[23] 1 John 3:8; John 12:31; 16:11; Heb. 2:14.

[24] Jesus's miracles demonstrate this, as do all of his symbolic statements about the inherent natures of the two kingdoms: one life-giving, and the other life-taking.

[25] Frank Viola, *Insurgence: Reclaiming the Gospel of the Kingdom* (Baker Books, 2018), 475, Kindle.

[26] In the Bible, the expressions "kingdom of God" and "kingdom of heaven" refer to the same thing. We know this for several reasons: (1) the different Gospel writers use them both to describe the same sayings of Jesus; (2) Matthew himself uses them interchangeably in 19:23-24; and (3) the Gospel writer who used the expression "kingdom of heaven" almost exclusively (Matthew) was writing to the Jews, many of whom used "heaven" as a circumlocution for "God" out of respect for the commandment in Exodus 20:7 to "not misuse the name of the Lord your God."

[27] Luke 4:43; 8:1; 16:16; Matt. 4:23; 9:35; 24:14.

[28] As Ronald J. Sider notes, "There is almost universal agreement among New Testament scholars today that the core of Jesus's proclamation was the 'gospel of the kingdom.'" See *Just Politics: A Guide for Christian Engagement* (Brazos Press, 2012), 1106, Kindle.

Stanley Hauerwas concurs with Sider's assessment: "there is widespread agreement that one of the most significant 'discoveries' of recent scholarship is that Jesus's teaching was not first of all focused on his own status but on the proclamation of the kingdom of God." See *The Peaceable Kingdom: A Primer in Christian Ethics* (Notre Dame, IN: University of Notre Dame Press, 1991), 73.

[29] Matt. 5:1-12, 19-20; 7:21; 11:11; 18:1-5; 21:31-32, 43; Mark 10:15; Luke 7:28; 18:17; John 3:3-5.

[30] Acts 1:1-3.

[31] John Howard Yoder, *The War of the Lamb: The Ethics of Nonviolence and Peacemaking*, ed. Glen Stassen, Mark Thiessen Nation, and Matt Hamsher (Brazos Press, 2009), 607, Kindle.

[32] Lee C. Camp, *Mere Discipleship: Radical Christianity in a Rebellious World* 2nd Edition (Brazos Press, 2008), 1637, Kindle.

[33] The New Testament says the cross was the means by which God demonstrated his love for us, forgave our sins, atoned for our sins, redeemed us, reconciled us to himself and others, made us righteous, gave us eternal life, defeated evil, and freed us from slavery to sin. See Rom. 3:24-25; 5:8-11, 15-19; 6:6-7; 8:1-3; John 1:29; 3:16; Eph. 1:7-8; 2:14-16; 5:1-2, 25; Gal. 2:20-21; 3:13-14; 6:14; Col 1:19-22; 2:13–15; 1 John 4:10; 1 Pet. 1:18-19; 2:24-25; 3:18; 1 Cor. 15:3; 2 Cor. 5:14-21; 13:4; Heb. 2:14-15; 9:28.

[34] To learn more about this aspect of what Jesus was doing on and through the cross, check out the Christus Victor theory of the atonement.

[35] Col. 2:15; Heb. 2:14-15.

[36] See also Rev. 17:14; 19:16.

[37] N. T. Wright, *How God Became King: The Forgotten Story of the Gospels* (HarperOne, 2012), 792, Kindle.

[38] Ibid., 792 and 2798.

[39] Ibid., 792 and 734.

[40] Ibid., 2738.

[41] N. T. Wright, *Simply Jesus: A New Vision of Who He Was, What He Did, and Why He Matters* (HarperCollins, 2011), 2562, Kindle.

[42] To explain it another way, an awareness of the different kingdom periods resolves the Bible's seemingly contradictory use of near, present, and future tenses to describe its timing and presence.

43 Matt. 13:36-43, 25:31-46; 2 Pet. 3:10-13; 1 Cor. 15:24-26; Rom. 16:20; Rev. 11:15; 20:10, 14.

44 Rev. 21:4.

45 Rev. 12:12.

46 C. S. Lewis, *Mere Christianity*, 46.

47 Charles H. Spurgeon, *Devotional Classics of C. H. Spurgeon: Morning & Evening I & II*, Volume I of *The Fifty Greatest Christian Classics* (Lafayette, IN: Sovereign Grace Publishers, Inc., 1990), 209.

48 See also 1 Thess. 5:8.

49 In addition to the verses cited above, see also the relatively well-known analogy in Luke 14:31.

50 Hays, *The Moral Vision of the New Testament*, 9268.

51 Guy Franklin Hershberger, *War, Peace, and Nonresistance* 5th Edition (Scottdale, PA: Herald Press, 2009), 306-307.

52 Gorman, *Reading Revelation Responsibly*, 480.

CHAPTER 3
THE AUDIENCE AND THEIR PROBLEM

Another key to properly interpreting any writing is understanding its intended audience and purpose. To whom was it written and why?

Authored by a first-century Christian living in political exile, Revelation was written to address the political crisis faced by the early church, which was a minority group struggling with how to remain faithful to Jesus's kingship while living amid a competing empire. Roman society was pressuring the early Christians to conform and compromise. It was telling them to be good Roman citizens, to acquiesce to the supremacy of the nation. It was urging them to fall in line like everyone else, to support the empire's systems of power and domination (through everyday loyalty, and occasional contributions of time and money) and to participate in its growing emperor cult (through taking part in its rituals and festivals designed to promote the worship of Caesar).

Do these things, said Rome, or suffer the consequences. Become productive, contributing members of the Roman Empire and enjoy the relative safety, comfort, and control it provides or remain faithful to the subversive, anti-power kingship of Jesus and suffer the social, economic, and political repercussions. Go through the patriotic motions and live a normal life or resist such idolatry and endure constant civil discomfort and occasional public mistreatment—maybe even death. In short, compromise and avoid persecution, or remain faithful and suffer it. This was the early church's quandary.

Look at what Revelation says to the seven churches. While each receives a message tailored to its own unique situation, the overarching issue is always about remaining faithful and avoiding compromise. The churches in Ephesus, Pergamum, Thyatira, and Philadelphia are all praised for persevering and enduring hardship and abuse, while the church in Smyrna is encouraged to remain faithful during its impending persecution.[1] Three of those churches—Ephesus, Pergamum, and Thyatira—are also chastised for their acts of unfaithfulness, from forsaking love to accepting false teachings that lead to idolatry.[2] The church in Sardis is generally criticized for not holding fast to God's teachings, while those few members who have held true are applauded.[3] The church in Laodicea is not praised for anything but is instead condemned for accumulating wealth to become self-sufficient, just like empires do.[4]

When we read these messages to the seven churches, Gorman observes, "we are struck by two major problems that the churches are confronting: the reality of various kinds of persecution, and the strong temptation to accommodate, with accommodation perhaps being seen by some as the way to avoid or stop persecution."[5]

The sheer amount of discussion about faithfulness in Revelation is overwhelming once you know to look for it. John sets the tone from the start: beyond identifying himself as a servant of God, the only other thing he says about himself is that he is someone who has patiently endured suffering for God's kingdom.[6] And in addition to the faithfulness-centered messages to the churches at the beginning of Revelation, further calls for faithfulness and patient endurance occur throughout the book.[7] Numerous times, God's followers are even explicitly commanded to remain faithful *unto death*, and are then praised for doing so.[8] Similarly, the faithful are repeatedly promised rewards while the unfaithful are repeatedly warned of judgment.[9]

It's easy to see how empire fits into this faithfulness equation. We need only ask ourselves, "Who is doing the persecuting, and why?" Who: the Roman Empire. Why: because the church is refusing to grant it supremacy.

Throughout Revelation, empire is God's enemy. The whole book is one big battle between his kingdom and earthly kingdoms, and its entire narrative portrays empire as Satan's primary tool, the predominant means by which he effectuates his earthly reign and opposes God's kingdom and its followers. Numerous times, John explicitly states that earthly rulers are under Satan's deceptive and seductive control and influence.[10] They receive their power from him, they worship him, and they are used by him to wage war on God's people.[11] Empire is, according to Revelation, public enemy number one.

What Revelation says about the two beasts and Babylon bears this out. Let's start with the beasts. The first half of Revelation talks a lot about God's kingdom conquering, but it doesn't specify who or what needs to be conquered. At the midway point, in Chapters 12 and 13, we get our answer: the evil trinity, which comprises the dragon (Satan) and his two underling beasts. For numerous reasons, almost all biblical scholars agree that the first beast, the one from the sea, represents the Roman Empire specifically and imperial power more generally.[12] Similarly, the second beast, the one from the earth, symbolizes the supporters and promoters of imperial power, from high-level government officials to local elites and lowly bureaucrats. The description of the second beast's actions in 13:11-17 makes this clear. So the first beast is empire and the second its minions.

Now consider what Revelation says about the beasts. "The dragon gave the beast his power and his throne and great authority.... The whole world was filled with wonder and followed the beast. People worshiped ... the beast and asked, 'Who is like the beast? Who can wage war against it?'" (13:2-4). "[The beast] opened its mouth to blaspheme God, and to slander his name and his dwelling place and those who live in heaven. It was given power to wage war against God's holy people and to conquer them. And it was given authority over every tribe, people, language and nation" (13:6-7). The beast sent forth demonic spirits to perform signs and "go out to the kings of the whole world, to gather them for the battle on the great day of God Almighty" (16:13-14). "The beast and the kings of the earth and their armies gathered together to wage war against the rider on the horse and his army" (19:19). They joined forces to "wage war against the Lamb" but Jesus will "triumph over them" (17:14). Ultimately, "the beast was captured" and "thrown alive into the fiery lake of burning sulfur" where he "will be tormented day and night for ever and ever" (19:19-20; 20:10). Then those who "had not worshiped the beast or its image and had not received its mark on their foreheads or their hands ... came to life and reigned with Christ a thousand years" (20:4). As you can see, the beast (earthly empire) and God's kingdom (including Jesus and his followers) don't much care for each other.

What Revelation says about Babylon sends the same message. Specifically, Babylon symbolizes the city of Rome.[13] More generally, it represents the fruit of empire, a great city of wealth and power built upon the violent control, domination, and exploitation of others. (When John first sees Babylon in 17:3-5, it is riding the first beast.) Babylon is, according to the symbolism of Revelation, the center and epitome of Satan's kingdom and his violent means of ruling.

No wonder Revelation says such harsh things about it. It calls Babylon "the great mother of prostitutes and of the abominations of the earth" and "the great prostitute who corrupted the earth by her adulteries" (17:5; 19:2). "With her the kings of the earth committed adultery, and the inhabitants of the earth were intoxicated with the wine of her adulteries" (17:2).[14] "The merchants of the earth grew rich from her excessive luxuries" (18:3). She gave herself "glory and luxury" and boasted of her power (18:7). She became "drunk with the blood of God's holy people, the blood of those who bore testimony to Jesus" (17:6; 18:24). God's followers are explicitly called to "come out of her, my people, so that you will not share in her sins, so that you will not receive any of her plagues" (18:4). When Babylon is defeated, those who mourn are "the kings of the earth who committed adultery with her and shared her luxury" and "the merchants of the earth" who amassed wealth under her reign (18:9-19). Those who rejoice are God's people, particularly those that were slaughtered by her, and they rejoice alongside the heavenly assembly.[15] Babylon, the center and epitome of empire, is, to put it mildly, no friend of God's. It misleads, oppresses, and destroys his creation.

These anti-empire themes, so blatantly revealed in the beasts and Babylon, permeate Revelation. Throughout the book, the behavior of empire is continually contrasted with faithfulness to God. Repeatedly, the ways of empire are associated with evil, sin, and disobedience. The whole book declares the entire system of empire—its politics, its economics, its religion, etc.—to be of Satan and directly in conflict with God's kingdom and Jesus's kingship.

The two kingdoms are incompatible. Allegiance to empire is antithetical to allegiance to God; the worship of Caesar precludes the worship of God; and trust in imperial power is at odds with trust in God.

We cannot serve two masters or enlist in competing armies. We must decide whose way of living and ruling we will adopt and cultivate, whose version of reality we will embrace and embody. Will it be the power politics of earthly governments, or the servant kingship of Jesus? Will we align ourselves with the world's rulers who excel at violently imposing their will on others, or with the slaughtered lamb who self-sacrificially loves others even unto death? We must choose between the civil religion of empire and discipleship in Christ.

According to Revelation, empire is an idol, a competitor god. Empire demands that we worship it, while God insists that we worship him alone.[16] Empire calls us to acknowledge its supreme rule, while God declares Jesus to be the world's rightful ruler.[17] Empire claims that it is in control and will win, while God assures us of his own control and inevitable victory.[18] God even declares that those who remain faithful to him, those who avoid complicity with earthly nations, will someday be given authority to rule over those same nations.[19]

As you've likely noticed by now, Revelation paints earthly rulers in a much different light than some other New Testament passages. There is no hint of government being God's servant for humanity's good; humble submission to it is nowhere encouraged; and honor is the last thing it is due. Revelation leaves no room for compromise or complacency. What it demands instead is an ethic of opposition. "Revelation is above all else a political resistance document," writes Hays. "It refuses to acknowledge the legitimacy and authority of earthly rulers and looks defiantly to the future, when all things will be subjected to the authority of God."[20]

Revelation reflects the reality that human government usually, if not always, oversteps its limited God-ordained role and asserts itself as a savior—as the provider, protector, and hope of the world, not to mention the driver of history. This is why the book is, as Gorman observed, "a sustained stripping of the sacred from secular power—military, political, economic—and a parallel sustained recognition of God and the Lamb as the rightful bearers of sacred claims, the only worthy recipients of divine accolades."[21]

Again, the issue Revelation addresses is not when or how the world will end, but how Christians should react to the temptations of earthly power. Does God really want us to refrain from participating in the secular religion of safety, comfort, and control, particularly at the cost of persecution, or can we make some seemingly harmless compromises to avoid seemingly unnecessary suffering? Does strict faithfulness really matter? Does it make a difference? Does it contribute to God's victory? Or are Christians wasting their lives by following the crucified Christ instead of the world's power brokers, who appear to be in control? This was the dilemma facing the first-century church.

Revelation provides a clear and emphatic answer to these questions: Don't compromise! Not even one iota! Remain faithful, even when it seems ineffective! And if necessary, hold steady even unto death! By doing so, you are taking back territory for God. You are helping Jesus rule the world. You are defeating Satan and his minions. Be assured, God is in control and this is how he has chosen to restore creation—through you, through your faithful embodiment of his radically nonviolent kingdom, as exemplified by his pacifistic, self-sacrificial, crucified Son.

In this sense, Revelation encourages faithfulness in two ways: by comforting the afflicted and afflicting the comfortable.[22] The faithful who were suffering persecution needed reassurance that God was in control, encouragement to remain steadfast, and hope that it was all worth it. On the other hand, those who were getting too cozy with empire needed to be warned of the negative consequences of doing so and challenged to repent and correct course.

This explains Revelation's frequent and severe warnings about God's judgment and ultimate victory. Those warnings accomplish both purposes: by sending the message that God hates, judges, and will eventually eradicate injustice, they offer hope to those suffering under empire's oppression and caution to those flirting with it, and rouse those already sharing its bed. The more frequently and graphically Revelation conveys and communicates this message of God's justice, the more effectively it accomplishes those aims.

This also explains Revelation's recurring promises of eternal rewards for the faithful. They provide encouragement, motivation, and hope by reassuring God's followers that their suffering is temporary, that death doesn't have the final word, that God will eventually restore all creation to its original state of harmony, and that the faithful will partake in that harmony, forever. Although Revelation is known more for its diatribes against injustice and unfaithfulness, it talks almost as much about the rewards for doing justice and remaining faithful. For those who believe in and yearn for God's justice, it is an immensely hopeful book.

Revelation's motivational message—remain faithful and reap the rewards or compromise and suffer the consequences—is good news for some and sobering news for others. Either way, however, it's all about promoting faithfulness.

This is what biblical prophecy does. It speaks words of comfort and challenge to God's people. As such, Revelation's "visions of the future," notes Gorman, "are not an end in themselves but rather a means—both to warn and to comfort."[23]

Leave it to us comfortable Westerners residing in—and dutifully supporting—the largest, most powerful government the world has ever seen to ignore (or worse, misappropriate) Revelation's words of comfort, assume its words of challenge apply to everyone but ourselves, and read the book not as a critique of empire, violence, and complacency but as a puzzle book of literal, end-time actors and events designed for our decoding entertainment.

---

[1] Rev. 2:2-3, 10, 13, 19, 24; 3:8, 10.

[2] Rev. 2:4, 14-15, 20.

[3] Rev. 3:1-4.

[4] Rev. 3:17.

[5] Gorman, *Reading Revelation Responsibly*, 1904.

[6] Rev. 1:9.

[7] Rev. 1:3; 2:26; 6:9-11; 12:17; 13:10; 14:3-5, 12; 16:15; 17:14.

[8] Rev. 2:10; 12:11; 13:10; 14:13; 20:4, 6.

[9] Rev. 1:3; 2:4-5, 7, 11, 16-17, 26-28; 3:3-5, 10, 12, 21; 7:14-17; 11:18; 14:7, 9-11, 13; 16:1-21; 19:9; 20:4-6, 12-13; 21:3-8; 22:1-5; 22:7, 12, 14.

[10] Rev. 13:3-4, 14; 18:3, 23; 20:2-3, 7-10.

¹¹ Rev. 11:7; 13:2-4, 7, 8, 12; 16:5-6, 13-14, 16; 17:12-14; 19:19; 20:7-9.

¹² For example, in 17:9-14, John explains that the first beast's seven heads symbolize seven kings (five that are fallen, one that is, and one that is yet to come) and its ten horns symbolize an additional ten kings (who have yet to receive a kingdom).

¹³ As N.T. Wright bluntly states in his book *Revelation for Everyone*, "Anyone who knows anything about the book of Revelation knows that 'Babylon' is used as a symbol later in the book … where John without a shadow of doubt means 'Rome.'" See Kindle location 2272.

¹⁴ See also 14:8.

¹⁵ Rev. 18:20, 24; 19:1-8.

¹⁶ Rev. 13:8, 12, 15-17; 14:9-11; 16:1-2, 10-11; 20:14-15; 21:8.

¹⁷ Rev. 1:4-5; 2:26-27; 3:14; 11:15; 12:5; 17:14; 19:15-16.

¹⁸ Rev. 15:3-4; 21:24-27; 16:19; 17:12-14; 18:4-8, 21; 19:1-2, 15, 19-21; 20:10.

¹⁹ Rev. 2:26-27; 5:9-10; 20:4, 6; 22:5.

²⁰ Hays, *The Moral Vision of the New Testament*, 4803.

²¹ Gorman, *Reading Revelation Responsibly*, 1195.

²² This description is a paraphrase of a point Hays made in *The Moral Vision of the New Testament*. See Kindle location 4977.

²³ Gorman, *Reading Revelation Responsibly*, 581.

PART II
ANALYZING ITS VIOLENCE

CHAPTER 4
THE TRIUMPH OF THE SLAIN LAMB

Now that we've placed Revelation within its proper context, let's explore its primary antiviolence symbols and themes.

In the first scene of John's vision, we find ourselves in God's heavenly throne room, where he is surrounded by various heavenly attendants (elders, angels, and creatures) and is holding a scroll sealed with seven seals (5:1). When an angel asks who is worthy to break the seals and open it, no one is found in heaven or on earth who qualifies, causing John to weep (vv. 3-4). Inside the scroll is God's redemptive plan for human history, how he intends to save the world from evil (i.e., Satan's reign) and restore it to its originally created state of peace, joy, and harmony—and it appears doomed to remain locked. But then an elder says to John, "Do not weep! See, the Lion of the tribe of Judah, the Root of David, has triumphed. He is able to open the scroll and its seven seals" (v. 5). At once, John sees "a Lamb, looking as if it had been slain, standing at the center of the throne" (v. 6). The creatures and elders begin worshipping the Lamb, singing, "You are worthy to take the scroll and to open its seals, because you were slain, and with your blood you purchased for God persons from every tribe and language and people and nation" (v.9). Then thousands of angels surround the throne and begin proclaiming, "Worthy is the Lamb, who was slain, to receive power and wealth and wisdom and strength and honor and glory and praise!" (v. 12). After that, the scene shifts as we watch the Lamb open each seal.

Most biblical scholars agree that this scene is the central and centering vision of the entire book, the interpretive key to everything else in it, including all the strange visions that follow. This is as it should be. The declaration that the slaughtered lamb (who is obviously Jesus!) is alone worthy to open the scrolls places him at center stage, right where he belongs. His sacrificial death on the cross is the center point of the entire Bible, the event around which everything else revolves.

John also stresses Jesus's primacy in numerous other ways throughout Revelation. He begins the book by declaring it to be a revelation from and about Jesus.[1] He claims that Jesus, along with God, is the source of salvation[2] and declares him to be "the First and the Last," the "Living One" who holds "the keys of death and Hades" (1:5, 17-18). Jesus is, in fact, depicted opening each of the seven seals, thereby unleashing God's judgment on evil, his final victory over Satan, and the reestablishment of his eternal kingdom on earth as it is in heaven. Such a sequence culminates in John proclaiming, "The kingdom of the world has become the kingdom of our Lord and of his Messiah, and he will reign for ever and ever" (11:15). At other points in the book, Jesus battles, defeats, and is declared ruler over the beast and his army of earthly kings.[3] When Babylon is defeated, a voice declares "the wedding of the *Lamb* has come" (19:7). John calls God's restored creation, the New Jerusalem, "the wife of the *Lamb*," a city whose foundation is "the twelve apostles of the *Lamb*" (21:9, 14). And only those whose names are written in the "*Lamb's* book of life" are allowed into it (21:27). Likewise, when Eden is restored at the end of Revelation, God's throne is referred to as "the throne of God and of the *Lamb*" (22:1, 3). John even defines God's followers as those who remain faithful to Jesus, follow him wherever he goes, and conquer as he conquers.[4] The evidence goes on, but you get the point: Jesus is key.

Notice the nonviolence implications of this opening scene. At the heart of God's salvation plan, the key to unlocking the meaning and purpose and aim of human history, is not a slaughtering lion but a slaughtered lamb. The elder introduces the one who "has triumphed" as "the Lion of the tribe of Judah," but when John looks he sees "a Lamb, looking as if it had been slain" (5:5-6). Shockingly, the Messiah, the central character in all of history, turns out not to be a lion but a harmless, defenseless, nonviolent lamb— and a slain one at that. N.T. Wright calls this "one of the most decisive moments in all scripture. What John has *heard* is the announcement of the lion. What he then *sees* is the lamb."[5] Similarly, Eugene Boring labels it "one of the most mind-wrenching and theologically pregnant transformations of imagery in literature."[6] After this symbolic redefinition, John never again refers to God's great conqueror as a lion—only a lamb.

This surprise echoes the surprise of the Gospels. They say, "Surprise! The anticipated militaristic messiah is actually a vulnerable pacifist!" Revelation says, "Surprise! The conquering lion is actually a slaughtered lamb!"

Furthermore, this scene declares Jesus's nonviolent self-sacrifice essential to his ability to open the scrolls. Notice why both the elders and angels proclaim him worthy to do so: "You are worthy to take the scroll and to open its seals, *because you were slain*," and "Worthy is the Lamb, *who was slain*." So not only is the lowly servant Jesus key, which is shocking in itself, but he is key *because* he was slain! To put it in terms of violence, Jesus possessed the ability to unlock God's plan because he lovingly absorbed violence, not because he wielded it in a more just way.

This whole scene is a direct assault on the notion of redemptive violence. It confirms the gospel message that God conquers through uncompromising, nonviolent, self-sacrificial love, not through a superior ability to wield force. Violence does not redeem or save; Christlike love does. Violence is not the most powerful force in the universe; Christlike love is.

All of this affirms my earlier point that Revelation, particularly what it says about Jesus, must be read through the lens of the Gospels, not vice versa. The Gospels present a historical account of the real-life Jesus—of how he lived, what he taught, and how he conquered evil. Revelation simply presents a symbolic, dreamlike vision of Jesus. Interpreting more obscure, more symbolic passages through clearer, more literal passages is fundamental to proper literary interpretation. Therefore, we must interpret Jesus's symbolic actions in Revelation through his literal actions in the Gospels—not vice versa.

Revelation's first two verses set the reader up to do precisely this. By declaring itself to be the revelation of and from Jesus, the book orients the reader toward what she already knows about Jesus from his actual life. Plus, as Hays points out, "The image of the triumphant 'Lamb that was slaughtered' is unintelligible apart from the Gospel narratives of Jesus's crucifixion and resurrection."[7] So is Revelation's claim that Jesus has *already* triumphed (3:21; 5:5), which only makes sense if the reader already knows Jesus's life story.

When we interpret Revelation from this proper perspective, it becomes clear that Jesus's actions in Revelation, even those that are widely believed to be undeniably violent, are entirely consistent with his nonviolent actions in the Gospels. Let's take a look in the next few chapters.

---

[1] Rev. 1:1-2. As Vernard Eller explains in his commentary *The Most Revealing Book of the Bible: Making Sense Out of Revelation*, when John introduces his letter as "the revelation from Jesus Christ," he intends it to convey two points. He wants Jesus "to be understood as the Revealer, the prime possessor and bearer of the revelation," and also "the content of the revelation. Jesus Christ is both the Revealer and that which is being revealed." See page 12.

[2] Rev. 7:10; 12:10.

[3] Rev. 1:5; 17:14; 19:13-21.

[4] Rev. 12:11, 17; 14:4-5, 12; 17:6, 14-17; 19:10, 13-14; 20:4, 6.

[5] N. T. Wright, *Revelation for Everyone*, 1008.

[6] M. Eugene Boring, "Narrative Christology in the Apocalypse," CBQ 54, no. 4 (1992): 708.

[7] Richard B. Hays, *Revelation and the Politics of Apocalyptic Interpretation*, ed. Richard B. Hays and Stefan Alkier (Baylor University Press, 2012), 1854, Kindle.

CHAPTER 5

JESUS WAGING WAR ON A WHITE HORSE

We begin our examination of Jesus's actions in Revelation with the book's most famous depiction of a supposedly violent Jesus. Here's the passage:

> I saw heaven standing open and there before me was a white horse, whose rider is called Faithful and True. With justice he judges and wages war. His eyes are like blazing fire, and on his head are many crowns. He has a name written on him that no one knows but he himself. He is dressed in a robe dipped in blood, and his name is the Word of God. The armies of heaven were following him, riding on white horses and dressed in fine linen, white and clean. Coming out of his mouth is a sharp sword with which to strike down the nations. "He will rule them with an iron scepter." He treads the winepress of the fury of the wrath of God Almighty. On his robe and on his thigh he has this name written: king of kings and lord of lords.

> And I saw an angel standing in the sun, who cried in a loud voice to all the birds flying in midair, "Come, gather together for the great supper of God, so that you may eat the flesh of kings, generals, and the mighty, of horses and their riders, and the flesh of all people, free and slave, great and small."

> Then I saw the beast and the kings of the earth and their armies gathered together to wage war against the rider on the horse and his army. But the beast was captured, and with it the false prophet who had performed the signs on its behalf. With these signs he had deluded those who had received the mark of the beast and worshiped its image. The two of them were thrown alive into the fiery lake of burning sulfur. The rest were killed with the sword coming out of the mouth of the rider on the horse, and all the birds gorged themselves on their flesh. (Rev. 19:11-21)

Interpreted literally, there's no doubt Jesus commits violence in this passage. But John didn't intend for this passage to be interpreted literally. Like the rest of his vision, everything in it is symbolic.

For starters, notice that Jesus's robe is bloody prior to his battle with the beast and kings. Given that he hasn't yet engaged the enemy and considering what we already know about Jesus from the Gospels (e.g., he only ever shed his own blood) and from his first appearance in John's vision (as an already slaughtered lamb), we should conclude the blood on Jesus's robe is his own, not that of his enemies.

This interpretation is consistent with all the other bloodshed in Revelation. Anytime shed blood is mentioned, it is always the blood of Jesus or his followers. With one possible exception, which we will analyze soon, Revelation never refers to blood that has been shed by God, Jesus, or their followers. As Preston Sprinkle notes, "God never causes His enemies to bleed in Revelation—literally or symbolically."[1] On the other hand, God's enemies cause his followers to bleed so thoroughly they are described as being drunk on blood.[2]

The fact that Jesus's heavenly army is "dressed in fine linen, white and clean" (v. 14) also indicates the blood on Jesus's robe is his own, not that of his enemies. As John has previously explained, the "fine linen stands for the righteous acts of God's holy people" (v. 8) and white robes represent those who "have washed their robes and made them white in the blood of the Lamb" (7:14). Indeed, white robes had already been given to "those who had been slain because of the word of God and the testimony they had maintained" (6:9-11). So according to Revelation itself, even Jesus's troops ride into battle having already been in contact with *his* blood and having already mimicked his *self*-sacrifice. Like Jesus, they engage the enemy with righteous acts, not with violent weapons, and they overcome by self-sacrificially shedding their own blood, not by making others bleed. As the voice from heaven puts it, they triumph "by the blood of the Lamb and by the word of their testimony" (12:11).

From this perspective, not only is the blood on Jesus's robe his own blood, but it symbolizes two important things about him, and consequently about his followers: it indicates he has *already* conquered via the cross, and it represents *how* he has conquered (and continues to conquer)—through the self-sacrificial shedding of his own blood. Revelation, not to mention the rest of the New Testament, makes these points over and over again in various ways. Sometimes Revelation even makes them simultaneously, like when it declares that Jesus "has freed us from our sins by his blood" (1:5) or proclaims that by his blood he "purchased for God persons from every tribe and language and people and nation" (5:9).

So yes, there's a lot of blood in Revelation, but it all flows from Jesus and his followers, not their enemies. And yes, the means by which Jesus and his followers conquer often involves the shedding of blood, but it's always their own blood. Therefore, when read through the lens of the Gospels and in the context of everything Revelation claims, the symbolic nature of the blood on Jesus's robe is clear: it is his own, not his enemies'.

Now consider the sword Jesus wields in this passage. Curiously, it comes out of his mouth. In fact, every time John depicts Jesus with a sword in Revelation, it is always protruding from his mouth.[3]

But why? What is John trying to communicate with such a placement? Why depict it coming out of his mouth instead of held in his hand?

Because John wants us to know the sword is symbolic, not literal. It's a metaphor. It represents something other than a literal sword. Had John wanted it to represent a literal sword, he would have, among other things, placed it in Jesus's hand.

This isn't the first time in Scripture we encounter a metaphorical sword associated with someone's mouth. On many occasions, the Psalmist referred to men whose tongues and words were sharp as swords.[4] Isaiah claimed that God had made his "mouth like a sharpened sword" (Isa. 49:2). He also prophesied that Jesus "will strike the earth with the rod of his mouth; with the breath of his lips he will slay the wicked" (Isa. 11:4). Even Jesus himself spoke of metaphorical swords: "Do not suppose that I have come to bring peace to the earth. I did not come to bring peace, but a sword" (Matt. 10:34).

The sword is not a sword. It's a symbol. Jesus no more literally wields a sword than he is literally a lamb with seven horns. Jesus is a man, not a lamb. And he wields a cross, not a sword.

So the sword is a symbol, but what does it symbolize? Generally, it symbolizes powerful speech. The sword signifies power, and its protrusion from the mouth signifies speech. In this specific situation, because the sword is coming out of *Jesus's* mouth, it symbolizes speaking God's truth. It has nothing to do with violence. It's about proclaiming the truth of and about God.

As if to remove any doubt about the symbolic nature and meaning of the sword, two verses before John mentions it, he declares that the name of the person whose mouth it protrudes from is "the Word of God" (v. 13). John isn't the only biblical writer to metaphorically correlate the Word of God with a sword. Here's the author of Hebrews: "For the word of God is alive and active. Sharper than any double-edged sword, it penetrates even to dividing soul and spirit, joints and marrow; it judges the thoughts and attitudes of the heart" (Heb. 4:12). And here's Paul: "Take the helmet of salvation and the sword of the Spirit, which is the word of God" (Eph. 6:17).

John sprinkled additional circumstantial evidence of this symbolic meaning throughout Revelation. For example, when we first meet Jesus in 1:16, he is holding seven stars representing the messengers of seven churches and has a sharp sword coming out of his mouth. He shows up on the scene equipped with a message of truth, not with weapons of violence. Similarly, in his instructions to the church of Pergamum, Jesus warns it to turn away from *false* teachers or he will "fight against them with the sword *of my mouth*" (2:14-16). He counters false teaching with truth telling.

Given that the heart of the biblical conflict between God and Satan centers on truth versus deceit, it makes sense that Jesus fights with the truth. This theme—God's truth versus Satan's deceit—goes all the way back to the Garden of Eden, where the serpent deceived Adam and Eve into believing that God's instructions were not for their good, and it continues all the way through Revelation.

In fact, this theme plays a prominent role in Revelation. God and Jesus are repeatedly referred to as truthful, as are their followers and those whom they allow into their kingdom. On the other hand, their adversaries include: a *false* prophet; a beast who is primarily described as a blasphemer and deceiver; the whorish Babylon, who is accused of leading the nations astray; and Satan, whose primary crime against humanity is deceiving it and who is eventually thrown into the Abyss to keep him from doing exactly that.[5] And remember, the whole point of the book of *Revelation* is to *reveal* the truth. Its title is the Greek word *apokalypsis*, which means an unveiling of truth. This is what biblical prophecy is all about, and it is why John's vision centers around him being given access to the heavenly control room. There, he is shown reality for what it truly is, in stark contrast to the deceptive view Satan perpetuates on earth.

So whose view of reality will you adopt? Satan's claim that violence-based earthly dominion is supremely powerful and effective or God's claim that Christlike love is? What weapon will you wield in your pursuit of good—redemptive violence or redemptive love?

At this point, you may be thinking, "Okay, you've convinced me that the bloody robe and protruding sword don't symbolize a violent Jesus, but what about all the other violence-related talk in this passage, like the reference to Jesus waging war, striking down the nations, ruling with an iron scepter, treading the winepress of God's wrath, throwing the beast and his cohorts into the fiery lake, and killing people with his mouth sword?" Good question. I'm glad you asked, because this is where things get really interesting.

The key to properly interpreting all the symbolism in this passage—and consequently, the key to realizing that none of its violence-related talk is intended to depict a violent Jesus—is understanding that John is simultaneously communicating two messages: (1) Jesus is at war, is powerful, and is a conqueror and (2) *how* Jesus wages war, exerts power, and conquers. Hence his seemingly contradictory mix of violent and nonviolent symbols. Let's take a quick look at how this dichotomy plays out.

First, in keeping with the biblical warfare worldview, John depicts Jesus at war with evil. This is no game. The struggle is real and the fate of the universe is at stake. So Jesus mounts a war horse, grabs his sword, gathers his army, and meets the enemy on the battlefield.

Second, Jesus hates injustice and intends to defeat it once and for all. He does not join the fight to become a martyr. He is in it to win it. He wields a sword to "strike down the nations" and aims to "rule them with an iron scepter." Earthly power brokers have defiled God's harmonious kingdom with injustice, and Jesus is livid: "He treads the winepress of the fury of the wrath of God Almighty."

Third, Jesus accomplishes his mission. He is victorious. He captures the beast and false prophet and throws them into the lake of fire. Then he uses his sword to kill the unjust kings of the earth and their armies.

These violence-related symbols exist to communicate that Jesus hates injustice, is at war with it, and will conquer it. Given the suffering God's followers were enduring, John is reassuring them that Jesus's seemingly ineffective way of fighting evil with nonviolent self-sacrificial love is not only effective but so powerful it will eventually eradicate evil. The entire book of Revelation is nothing less than an apocalyptic confirmation of exactly that.

In other words, the "striking down" and "killing" in this passage symbolize Jesus's victory and evil's defeat, not literal violence. After all, the nations that are destroyed in this passage reappear alive and well in numerous passages later.[6] So when John writes, "the rest were killed with the sword coming out of the mouth of the rider on the horse," he intends to communicate that Jesus conquers through truth, not that he literally kills people with a magic sword protruding from his mouth. Yes, Jesus will triumph over the unjust nations, he will defeat the beast and his minions, and he will vanquish those who persist in unloving behavior— but he won't do so with violence.

In short, the literal element of these violence-related depictions of Jesus is that he fights and conquers, not *how* he does so. These images demonstrate the existence of Jesus's power, not the type of power he possesses. They portray the fact of his victory, not his means of victory.

To determine *how* Jesus fights and defeats evil, we must look to the other symbolic details in this passage (and interpret them through the lens of the Gospels). We've already done this with Jesus's robe dipped in blood *prior to battle*, the sword *coming out of his mouth*, and his being named the *Word* of God, all of which symbolize nonviolent means. There's one more detail worth mentioning.

Although the passage describes Jesus riding out to wage war and the beast and kings of the earth gathering to oppose him, no actual battle is described. John moves directly from describing both parties readying themselves for battle to declaring that the beast and false prophets have been captured and disposed of, along with their followers (vv. 19-21). Jesus's final battle with evil turns out to be not much of a battle at all.[7]

So why doesn't John see or describe a battle? Because the battle has already been fought and won via Jesus's life, death, and resurrection![8] In Vernard Eller's words, "Jesus did the fighting on Good Friday; God confirmed the victory on Easter."[9] There's no need for another battle. John need not depict Jesus shedding his enemies' blood because Jesus has already struck the fatal blow by shedding his own blood.

The only thing left to do is for Jesus (and his followers) to bear witness to his already-won victory, a victory that was achieved entirely through nonviolent, self-sacrificial love. This is why Jesus is only armed with a sword coming out of his mouth. To finish off his enemy, he need only speak the truth about what he has already accomplished. He need only remain "Faithful and True," which is what John calls the rider on the white horse (v. 11).

John doesn't describe a battle because he knows that the true enemy, deceit, can't be overcome with physical fighting—only with truth. As Paul put it, "we do not wage war as the world does" and our weapons "are not the weapons of the world" because "our struggle is not against flesh and blood, but against the rulers, against the authorities, against the powers of this dark world and against the spiritual forces of evil in the heavenly realms" (2 Cor. 10:3-4; Eph. 6:12). Consequently, we employ non-physical weapons like "the belt of truth … the breastplate of righteousness … the shield of faith … the helmet of salvation and the sword of the Spirit, which is the word of God" (Eph. 6:14-17). Unlike physical weapons, such things "have divine power to demolish strongholds" by destroying "every pretension that sets itself up against the knowledge of God" (2 Cor. 10:4–5).

Jesus knew this. He knew that deceit is the primary poison and truth is the only antidote, which is why he embodied truth instead of employing violence in the Gospels. It's also why Revelation repeatedly portrays Jesus with a weapon that symbolizes truth (a sword coming out of his mouth) and why it declares that God's followers "triumphed over [Satan] ... by the word of their testimony" (12:11), not by wielding violence in more just and effective ways. Just as God spoke the universe into existence, he will, in a way, speak evil out of existence. That's the only way to do it. Physical fighting is futile.

Here's another reason John doesn't describe a battle: This passage is primarily about communicating *that* Jesus conquers, not *how* he conquers. How Jesus conquers was already well-known by John's audience. They knew all about the scandalously nonviolent, slaughtered lamb. So John is writing not to re-explain Jesus's ethics but to assure his readers that Jesus's seemingly powerless ethics are, in reality, supremely powerful.

To summarize, the key to realizing that none of the violence-related talk in this passage, or anywhere else in Revelation, is intended to depict a violent Jesus is separating the symbols that demonstrate the fact that Jesus is at war, is powerful, and is a conqueror from the symbols that demonstrate *how* he wages war, exerts power, and conquers. Jesus's riding a war horse, wielding a sword, ruling with an iron scepter, treading the winepress of God's wrath, striking down the nations, killing with his mouth sword, and throwing the beast into the fiery lake all symbolize his very real battle with and victory over evil. Jesus's robe being bloodied before battle, the sword being placed in his mouth, his name being the Word of God, and the absence of a physical battle all symbolize the *means* by which he wages war against and triumphs over evil.

In terms of symbolically depicting a nonviolent victory over evil, you could do much worse than this scene. Consider how difficult it is to portray nonviolent fighting and conquering. Even with the recent development of nonviolent tactics of resistance and numerous contemporary examples of successful nonviolent campaigns (e.g., Gandhi and Martin Luther King, Jr.), our fallen minds still equate fighting and conquering with violence. To wage war, to do battle, and to defeat the enemy is to use violence. To not use violence is, in most people's minds, to do nothing. All of this would have been even truer of John's first-century audience.

But if Jesus really does fight and conquer evil, then that fighting and conquering has to be depicted somehow. And if Jesus also really does fight and conquer nonviolently, then his fighting and conquering also has to be depicted in a way that doesn't betray his nonviolence.

This scene resolves the dilemma quite nicely by drawing the perfect balance between symbolizing a literal victory and symbolizing the counterintuitively nonviolent means of that victory. Sure, the symbols of victory are arguably more prominent than the symbols of means, but that's because the book's primary aim was to reassure the early Christians of God's power and control. Despite how dominant and unconquerable earthly power (in the form of Rome) appeared, they needed to be reminded that God's counterintuitive way of ruling (as demonstrated by Jesus) has won, is winning, and will win. So John's symbolic vision stresses the victory over its means, but it also includes enough means-related details to affirm what his readers already knew about Jesus's nonviolent modus operandi. Can you think of a better way to symbolically and metaphorically depict Jesus's nonviolent victory over his violent enemies than to portray him "killing" them with a sword *from his mouth*?

We must continually fight the fallen urge to selectively interpret all of Revelation's nonviolent images metaphorically and all of its violent images literally. When John writes, "the rest were killed with the sword coming out of the mouth of the rider on the horse" (19:21), it's contradictory to conclude that the killing is literal but the sword is figurative. They are both figurative.

Nothing in John's vision is literal. Just as Satan isn't literally a dragon, Babylon isn't literally a prostitute for hire, and a seven-headed beast won't literally emerge from the sea to kill Christians, Jesus isn't literally a seven-eyed lamb, doesn't literally tread a winepress owned by God, and won't literally regurgitate a sword while riding a flying horse.

Everything in John's vision is communicated symbolically. Instead of mentioning Jesus's death on a cross, John symbolizes it in a slaughtered lamb. Likewise, instead of explaining how Jesus fought evil when he walked the earth, John symbolizes it by clothing him in a robe dipped in his own blood and placing a sword in his mouth.

What's true about Revelation's symbols is the immaterial message they are trying to communicate, not the material representation they employ to do so. Jesus isn't truly a lamb, but he is truly like one in his harmlessness, his nonviolence, and his vulnerability. He doesn't truly wage violent war—he doesn't truly grab a sword, mount a horse, and kill people—but he does truly fight and defeat injustice. We must not lose sight of the distinction between literal truth and symbolic truth.

Before we move on to looking at two other passages popularly believed to portray a violent end-times Jesus, I want to point out one more massive advantage of this nonviolent interpretation of Jesus waging war on a white horse: it is consistent with everything else the New Testament, including Revelation, says about how Jesus behaved and taught his followers to behave. Three quick examples should suffice.

First, it is consistent with Revelation's own description of Jesus as a triumphant lion *and* a slaughtered lamb. In the sense we've been discussing them, they are not incompatible. On the contrary, they are both indispensable. Jesus fights evil with the ferocity and power of a lion, but his means of fighting resemble the nonviolent, vulnerable tactics of a lamb. He fights valiantly but not violently.

Second, it is consistent with how Revelation depicts God's followers conquering evil. We will explore what the book demands of Christians in more detail soon, but here's the gist: "They triumphed over him by the blood of the Lamb and by the word of their testimony" (12:11).

Lastly, and most importantly, it is consistent with how Jesus fought and conquered evil in the Gospels and on the cross. As I explain in *Jesus the Pacifist*, his life, teachings, and death were all entirely nonviolent. He bore nonviolent witness to the truth of self-sacrificial love. He did not coerce, control, or kill.

Interpreting this passage, or any passage in Revelation, as a depiction of a violent Jesus subverts everything he said and did in the Gospels. When Jesus returns, he will not abandon his uniqueness and become just another Caesar. As Brian D. McLaren has written, the Jesus that walked the earth was not "a fake-me-out Jesus pretending to be a peace-and-love guy, when really he was planning to come back and act like a proper Caesar, more of a slash-and-burn guy, brutal, willing to torture, and determined to conquer with crushing violence."[10] Jesus isn't going to admit that his first trip to earth failed, that his crucifixion and resurrection were insufficient, that love doesn't always win, and that what is really needed is superior violence. He will not acknowledge that, as his critics have said all along, pacifism is naïve, passive, cowardly, hypocritical, ineffective, and irresponsible. Nor will he replace his "unrealistic" nonviolent commands with more "realistic" just war principles. "Those who live by the sword will die by the sword" will not become "those who live by a more just sword will reign with me in eternity." Jesus won't recant what he taught about loving your enemies, turning the other cheek, and repaying evil with good. He will not redirect his followers to lay down their crosses and take up their machine guns. Instead, Jesus's second coming will be consistent with his first, pacifistic one.

Revelation does not present a sudden, last-minute reversal of Jesus's nonviolent tactics. It represents a symbolic demonstration of the real-life power and effects of such tactics.

Likewise, Revelation is not a surprise overturning of the clear biblical trend away from violence and toward nonviolence, a trend I've discussed elsewhere.[11] Instead, it's a symbolic affirmation of it. Zahnd elaborates:

> The saddest thing is that the adherents of this schizophrenic Jesus often seem to prefer the violent Jesus over the peaceable Jesus. At a basic level they essentially see the Bible like this: After a long trajectory away from the divine violence of the Old Testament culminating in Jesus renouncing violence and calling his followers to love their enemies, the Bible in its final pages abandons a vision of peace and nonviolence as ultimately unworkable and closes with the most vicious portrayal of divine violence in all of Scripture. In this reading of Revelation, the way of peace and love that Jesus preached during his life and endorsed in his death is rejected for the worn-out way of war and violence. When we literalize the militant images of Revelation we arrive at this conclusion: in the end even Jesus gives up on love and resorts to violence. Tragically, those who refuse to embrace the way of peace taught by Jesus use the symbolic war of Revelation 19 to silence the Sermon on the Mount.[12]

Again, we must interpret Revelation's symbolic Jesus through the lens of the Gospel's historical Jesus, not vice versa. John's visionary Jesus must not be allowed to contradict every other New Testament writer's real-life Jesus. A few obscure images in the Bible's most perplexing book do not trump "The Word [who] became flesh and made his dwelling among us" (John 1:14).

With this interpretive framework in mind, let's briefly look at two more passages in Revelation that are often cited as depicting a violent Jesus.

---

[1] Preston Sprinkle, *Fight: A Christian Case for Non-Violence* (David C. Cook, 2013), 2746, Kindle.

[2] Rev. 17:6; 18:24.

[3] Rev. 1:16; 2:16; 19:15, 21.

4 Ps. 57:4; Ps. 59:7; 64:3.

5 Rev. 2:24; 3:7, 9, 14; 6:10; 12:9; 13:1-6, 14; 14:5; 15:3; 16:7; 17:3; 18:23; 19:2, 9, 11, 20; 20:3, 7, 9-10; 21:5, 27; 22:6, 15.

6 Boyd explains: "Beyond the previously mentioned considerations regarding the symbolic nature of John's word-pictures, the symbolic nature of this macabre scene is made quite clear by the fact that though this passage depicts all nations as being defeated (Rev 19:15, 19) and all rebels as being devoured by birds (Rev 19:18, 21), we continue to read about these nations and rebels in subsequent chapters (Rev 20:8, 22:11). Indeed, we are even given some hope that the nations and rebels who are slain and devoured in Revelation 19 will eventually be redeemed (Rev 21:24–26, 22:2). While no one who persists in wickedness can enter the heavenly city, the gates of the city will never be shut (Rev 21:25, 27)." See *The Crucifixion of the Warrior God*, 13962.

7 Interestingly, the same is true for the "final battle" with the other human-led institution in Revelation: Babylon. When it is defeated, no actual fighting occurs. It simply self-destructs.

8 John made this clear way back in Chapter 5 when he declared Jesus worthy to open the scroll because he "has triumphed," a fact he reminds us of in this passage by pointing out Jesus's already bloody robe.

9 Vernard Eller, *The Most Revealing Book of the Bible: Making Sense Out of Revelation* (Grand Rapids, MI: Wm. B. Eerdmans Publishing Co., 1975), 32.

10 Brian D. McLaren, *A New Kind of Christianity: Ten Questions That Are Transforming the Faith*, Reprint Edition (HarperCollins, 2010), 2111, Kindle.

11 See the last chapter in my book *The Old Testament Case for Nonviolence*.

12 Zahnd, *Sinners in the Hands of a Loving God*, 2270.

CHAPTER 6

THE FOUR HORSEMEN AND THE WINEPRESS OF GOD'S WRATH

When Jesus opens the first four seals in Chapter 6 of Revelation, he unleashes the Four Horsemen of the Apocalypse, each of whom wreaks havoc on humanity (6:1-8). The first rides a white horse, holds a bow, and gallops "out as a conqueror bent on conquest" (v. 2).[1] Rider two sits atop a fiery red horse, wields a large sword, and has the "power to take peace from the earth and to make people kill each other" (v. 4). The third rides a black horse, holds a pair of scales, and sows economic exploitation (vv. 5-6). Rider four has a pale horse, is named Death, and possesses the power to kill a fourth of the earth by sword, famine, plague, and wild beast (v. 8). When Jesus opens the sixth seal, a great earthquake occurs, causing everyone to hide from "the wrath of the Lamb" (vv. 12-16).

There's no doubt that violence results from Jesus's opening of the seals. But Jesus does not employ that violence, either directly or indirectly. He *allows* it, as the passive language ("was given") used throughout these verses indicates. Permit me to explain.

God's plan for redeeming all creation involves allowing Satan to show his true colors and humankind's disobedience to run its natural course, one riddled with violence and destruction. In opening these scrolls, Jesus is revealing what the world is like under Satan's reign and man's rebellion. He is shouting, "Look! This is the type of existence Satan's way of life produces!"

This is a natural stage in fallen humanity's moral evolution. Before it will choose God's way, humanity first must be permitted to arrogantly go its own way and experience the bitter fruit of doing so. It must be allowed to suffer the painful failure of trying to achieve peace, harmony, and salvation through its own means and power, through violence. It must be given the opportunity to realize that it has a problem and is helpless to fix it. Before it will go to the doctor for help, humanity must first realize it has a fatal disease and cannot cure it alone. Before it will voluntarily embrace a savior, humanity must be made aware of its need for a savior.

This is how a non-coercive God persuades. He doesn't force anyone to obey him. He allows us to exercise our free will in rebellious ways and then suffer the negative consequences—while he simultaneously demonstrates the positive consequences of obedience through those communities who embody his way of life. And all along, he sends prophets to continually highlight the differences between the two approaches. This is how an always-loving God convinces humanity that his way, the way of uncompromising self-sacrificial love, is best for all creation.

In this passage, Jesus is not inflicting punishment or causing destruction. He's revealing the self-punishing, self-destructive effects of humanity's violence. By unleashing the violent riders, Jesus no more causes the violence they commit than parents cause the violence their children commit when they unleash them into the world through procreation.

Trampling the Winepress of God's Wrath

Although the following passage is notoriously difficult to interpret, we can safely rule out a violent Jesus.

> I looked, and there before me was a white cloud, and seated on the cloud was one like a son of man with a crown of gold on his head and a sharp sickle in his hand. Then another angel came out of the temple and called in a loud voice to him who was sitting on the cloud, "Take your sickle and reap, because the time to reap has come, for the harvest of the earth is ripe." So he who was seated

on the cloud swung his sickle over the earth, and the earth was harvested.

Another angel came out of the temple in heaven, and he too had a sharp sickle. Still another angel, who had charge of the fire, came from the altar and called in a loud voice to him who had the sharp sickle, "Take your sharp sickle and gather the clusters of grapes from the earth's vine, because its grapes are ripe." The angel swung his sickle on the earth, gathered its grapes and threw them into the great winepress of God's wrath. They were trampled in the winepress outside the city, and blood flowed out of the press, rising as high as the horses' bridles for a distance of 1,600 stadia. (Rev. 14:14-20)

Note the clear distinction between what Jesus ("the one like a son of man") does in the first paragraph and what the angel does in the second. Jesus harvests the earth, but he is not involved in the winepress of God's wrath. He throws nothing into it. The angel does that.

To reap a harvest, particularly one that is ripe, is a positive thing. It means to gather the good crop. As N.T. Wright contends, "there should be no doubt that this passage, describing the harvest and the vintage, is meant to be an occasion of great, uninhibited joy. We would need a huge amount of evidence to force us to say anything else."[2] So the symbolism in the first paragraph has nothing to do with condemnation or punishment. It's about Jesus gathering the faithful to abide with him in God's kingdom for eternity. The harvest is ripe because the time has come for God's followers to be saved.

The context surrounding this passage supports this conclusion. The preceding verses announce the fall of Babylon and the defeat of the beast's followers before declaring that God's followers will, from now on, find rest from their labor (vv. 8-13). Then we have our passage, wherein Jesus ushers God's followers into eternal life and the angel kicks Satan's followers out of God's city ("They were trampled in the winepress outside the city"). Immediately thereafter, we find the faithful in heaven singing songs of praise and victory (15:1-4).

Many other New Testament passages also positively reference a metaphorical harvest, sometimes even in a similar context. After witnessing crowds that were harassed and helpless, Jesus had compassion on them and told his disciples, "The harvest is plentiful but the workers are few. Ask the Lord of the harvest, therefore, to send out workers into his harvest field" (Matt. 9:36-38). In a parable, Jesus compared God's kingdom to a man who scatters seed on the ground, watches the soil produce grain by itself, and "as soon as the grain is ripe, he puts the sickle to it, because the harvest has come" (Mark 4:26-29). On another occasion, Jesus said to his disciples, "Open your eyes and look at the fields! They are ripe for harvest. Even now the one who reaps draws a wage and harvests a crop for eternal life" (John 4:35-36). Similarly, Paul urged the Galatians to "not become weary in doing good, for at the proper time we will reap a harvest if we do not give up" (Gal. 6:9). He also told the church in Rome he had planned to visit them "in order that I might have a harvest among you" (Rom. 1:13). And on numerous other occasions, New Testament writers referred to a "harvest of righteousness" (James 3:18; Heb. 12:11; 2 Cor. 9:10).

This is one reasonable way to interpret this challenging passage. Jesus performs the nonviolent job of gathering the faithful to abide with him in God's kingdom forever. The angel, meanwhile, performs the metaphorically violent job of banishing from God's kingdom all of those who persist in unloving behavior. In Eller's words, "It is a double harvest: a positive grain harvest of blessing and a negative grape (wine) harvest of 'wrath.'"[3]

Here's a slightly different interpretation to consider: Maybe those trampled in the winepress of God's wrath aren't his enemies but his followers. The passage doesn't specify who does the trampling or whose blood flows from the press.

If it is the blood of God's enemies, this is the only place in Revelation where the word *blood* is used to denote the blood of God's enemies, instead of his followers. The trampling occurs "outside the city," which may allude to where others crucified and shed Jesus's blood: "Jesus also suffered outside the city gate to make the people holy through his own blood" (Heb. 13:12). Everywhere else in Revelation, God's judgment is symbolically represented not in the act of crushing grapes but in making the wicked drink the wine of crushed grapes.[4] In other words, he directs his wrath not toward the crushed grapes but toward those who trample them. So maybe the trampled grapes are Christian martyrs (who are being harvested) and those who trample them are their killers. Christian self-sacrifice is, after all, one of Revelation's most prominent themes.

Don't be misled by Revelation's references to God's "wrath." It's one of his better characteristics. It means he hates evil and injustice. It means he loves his creation and wants to see it thrive and therefore despises everything that thwarts its flourishing, like violence, bloodshed, oppression, exploitation, deceit, envy, greed, idolatry, and death. If God didn't want everyone and everything to have life and have it abundantly, he wouldn't get angry at such unloving behaviors. Praise God for his wrath! It is an essential part of his goodness. And it only needs to be feared if you want to persist in acting unlovingly.

This is also true for God's judgment and punishment. They are good things. They mean God fights injustice. He judges it, punishes it, and sets it right. Praise God for his judgment and punishment! They arise from his love, not from some arbitrary, selfish, jealous, or vengeful bloodlust. What kind of God would he be if he didn't combat things like racism, theft, child abuse, slavery, rape, murder, and war?

But please don't jump to conclusions about how God's wrath, judgment, punishment, and correction operate on a metaphysical level. None of them necessarily require God's use of violence. As theologians like Greg Boyd have demonstrated, it is reasonable, rational, biblical, and theologically sound to conclude that God achieves such things not by directly imposing them himself but by turning evildoers over to the natural consequences of their injustice, by allowing such behaviors to run their natural course, by permitting the disobedient way of life to self-destruct.[5] So maybe God enforces justice not through direct intervention but by channeling human injustice, by ensuring that it, like all things, is put to work for good.[6] Maybe God designed the universe to work in such a way that sin is its own punishment. The Bible, including Revelation, contains an intriguing amount of supporting evidence for such a theory.

So yes, God and Jesus both get angry at injustice. They both judge it to be wrong. But neither their wrath nor their judgment symbolizes violence. Instead, they symbolize a hatred of violence. Furthermore, all throughout the Bible, only God—not Jesus or his followers—punishes injustice.[7] And even then, God doesn't necessarily act violently when doing so. Sure, he may "use" violence indirectly by channeling it, but as Paul pointed out, God uses "all things" in such a way (Rom. 8:28). To use something someone else does is not to do it yourself.

Whatever meaning you derive from this passage or however you interpret God's wrath in general, one thing is clear in this passage about trampling the winepress of God's wrath: Jesus doesn't use violence. Even if this weren't clear, we should never interpret a single ambiguous passage in a way that contradicts numerous other, clearer passages.

And with that, we've covered every scene in Revelation wherein Jesus is possibly violent. All other violence that may be attributed to God's team comes either from God himself or an angel. Jesus, who is our moral standard, only ever wields and fights with a sword from his mouth and only ever battles and defeats the beast and earthly kings. Satan and Babylon are disposed of by other means.

¹ Some interpreters have claimed that this first rider represents Jesus. I don't think so. First, the rider carries a bow, a weapon that is nowhere else in Scripture associated with Jesus. Second, such a conclusion doesn't fit with the fact that all the other riders represent forces of evil. Third, while the rider shares two symbolic details with Jesus (he wears a crown like Jesus and he rides out to conquer on a white horse as Jesus does later in Revelation), so does all evil. "Evil is not sheer ugliness but rather counterfeit beauty," writes Eller. "Evil comes through as a perverted, mirror image of the Good. And this is the explanation of its power and attractiveness." (See page 36 in *The Most Revealing Book of the Bible*.) Instead, I believe, in accordance with N.T. Wright, that the rider on the white horse most likely "symbolizes the conquering kings of the earth who have charged to and fro, overcoming mighty nations and claiming sovereignty (the 'crown') over them." (See Kindle location 1147 in *Revelation for Everyone*.) However, even if the first rider does represent Jesus, notice he does not commit any violence or sow any specific destruction. He merely rides "out as a conqueror bent on conquest."

² N. T. Wright, *Revelation for Everyone*, 2355.

³ Eller, *The Most Revealing Book of the Bible*, 143.

⁴ Rev. 14:10; 16:6; 17:6.

⁵ See Boyd's *The Crucifixion of the Warrior God: Interpreting the Old Testament's Violent Portraits of God in Light of the Cross*, or his less-academic version *Cross Vision: How the Crucifixion of Jesus Makes Sense of Old Testament Violence*.

⁶ Rom. 8:28.

⁷ Highly astute readers will note that although Jesus isn't the one who throws the grapes into the winepress of God's wrath in this passage (14:14-20), he does "tread the winepress of the fury of the wrath of God" in the part of Chapter 19 discussed above. I think there's a small but significant distinction between the two. In Chapter 19, where Jesus treads the winepress, no one is thrown into it and no blood flows from it. In other words, in Chapter 19, God's wrath does not get imposed. It does not take the form of punishment. Therefore, to say that Jesus treads the winepress of God's wrath without depicting any associated punishment is

simply to say that Jesus, like God, hates injustice, a fact we've just learned has nothing to do with using violence.

CHAPTER 7

WHAT REVELATION DEMANDS OF CHRISTIANS

Even if we interpret the actions of Jesus, God, and the angels literally and violently, nothing in Revelation instructs Christians to use violence or depicts them doing so. The opposite is true.

As discussed earlier, Revelation calls Christians to faithfulness, demanding that we remain obedient amidst the world's competing ideologies—particularly the ideology of empire—and do so even to the point of martyrdom, if necessary. This is how Christians "conquer" and become "victorious." "Be faithful, even to the point of death," commands God, "and I will give you life as your victor's crown" (2:10). To remain faithful is to conquer, and to conquer is to remain faithful.[1]

But this raises a question: Faithfulness to whom or to what? Well, to state the obvious, faithfulness to God and his will. That is to say, faithfulness to the way of Jesus, who perfectly revealed God and his will.

Revelation connects faithfulness to Jesus both implicitly and explicitly. Within the first five verses, John declares him to be "the faithful witness" (1:5), a fact he reiterates two more times (3:14; 19:11). Throughout the book, God's followers are referred to as those who "follow the Lamb wherever he goes" (14:4), who "remain faithful to Jesus" (14:12), and who bear testimony to and about Jesus (12:17; 17:6; 19:10; 20:4). Jesus promises to reward those who do *his* will (2:26). God's faithful follow Jesus, not God himself or the angels, into battle against the kings of the earth (17:14; 19:13-14). They triumph as Jesus triumphed (3:21), "by the blood of the Lamb and by the word of their testimony" (12:11). They earn a place in heaven by suffering like Jesus did (7:14-15; 20:4) and by having their "names written in the Lamb's book of life" (21:27).

In short, faithfulness is how God's followers fight and Jesus defines clearly what it means to be faithful. Therefore, we wage war on evil by remaining faithful to Jesus's commands and example. Again, Revelation is not about providing Christians with a decipherable guide map of end-time events, but rather about promoting discipleship in the lives of its readers—then and now.

Furthermore, to be faithful to the way of Jesus means to be faithful to what he taught and exemplified *in the Gospels*. It does not mean faithfulness to some new Jesus or some new ethics revealed in Revelation.

Revelation doesn't teach new ethics. It encourages obedience to what Jesus has already taught, which it assumes its readers already know. This is why it contains tons of conclusory admonitions to simply be faithful and obey but almost no explanatory ethical instructions.[2] Revelation doesn't command us to care for the poor, turn the other cheek, or love our enemies because it's written to people who already know that's what God wants them to do, and who only need to be encouraged to keep at it or prodded to get with it.

Revelation doesn't issue new marching orders. It commands us to follow existing orders. And to identify those orders, we need to look to Jesus's life and teachings as recorded in the rest of the New Testament, particularly the Gospels. This makes sense. To deduce how Jesus conquered and wants us to conquer, we need to analyze the historical account of his conquering.

Revelation is nonsensical unless Jesus's gospel actions are the standard of faithfulness. Had Jesus not already demonstrated faithfulness (during his time on earth) and had John not intended for those past actions to define faithfulness, then Revelation's admonitions to follow Jesus, coupled with its lack of explanation as to precisely what that means for our behavior, would be irrational. Revelation's repeated references to Jesus's faithfulness and victory in the past tense would also not make sense. The flawed logic would be akin to an Old Testament writer who commanded God's followers to be faithful to Jesus prior to Jesus's birth—before anyone knew what that meant or what ethics it required.

Plus, not every biblical writer can say everything. Many, including John in Revelation, build upon what has already been said and done. In this sense, John never intended for Revelation to be a treatise on ethics. Nonetheless, to the small extent that it contains explicit ethical instructions, they are located in the messages to the seven churches—not in John's visions—and they echo Jesus's gospel teachings, commanding things like love, faith, service, patience, and repentance.[3]

At this point, what Christlike faithfulness means for our use of violence should be clear. It manifests itself in an entirely nonviolent way of life.[4] (If you doubt this, read the rest of *Jesus the Pacifist*.)

As Revelation itself points out, Jesus triumphed by being slain, not by slaying. He conquered as a lamb, not a lion. He could unlock the scroll because he had been slaughtered, not because he had slaughtered. Instead of somehow employing violence more justly than his enemy, he refrained from violence altogether. Rather than forcefully resisting violence, he self-sacrificially absorbed it. He took up his cross, not a sword—or even a shield. He fought and won by dying for God's enemies, not by killing them. Instead of protecting his life at the expense of those who threatened him, he laid it down for them. He chose to have his own innocent blood shed—even to the point of death—rather than shed the blood of the guilty. He was willing to die for truth and justice and the advancement of God's kingdom on earth, but not to kill for those things. Jesus's response to violence was not more violence. It was self-sacrificial love.

Revelation calls God's followers to the same nonviolent faithfulness. It praises and promises rewards for the slain, not the slayers.[5] It encourages God's followers to absorb and endure violent persecution, not to retaliate in kind.[6] It instructs them to not fear death because Jesus has already conquered it and holds power over it.[7] Its models of faithfulness are those who suffered and died bearing living witness to the truth of Jesus's way of life, not those who died trying to violently combat evil.[8] It memorializes prophets and martyrs, not fallen soldiers.[9]

Revelation never depicts God's followers carrying weapons of any type, not even swords protruding from their mouths.[10] Instead, it portrays them wearing robes made white by Jesus's own blood, which is a symbol of faithful suffering and martyrdom.[11]

Look at the role of Christians in each of Revelation's figurative battles against God's enemies. They are never even symbolically depicted fighting the beast, earthly kings, the false prophet, Babylon, or the dragon. Instead, it is always God, Jesus, or an angel who does the metaphorical fighting and killing.[12] Christians are only ever portrayed as being persecuted by God's enemies and encouraged to endure it.[13] On the single occasion in which they are summarily declared to have defeated an enemy (the dragon), they are said to have "triumphed over him by the blood of the Lamb and by the word of their testimony; they did not love their lives so much as to shrink from death" (12:11). And the two times they are pictured with Jesus when he defeats his enemies, they are never depicted doing any actual fighting.[14] They simply follow Jesus "wherever he goes" (14:4).

Returning to Jesus's faithfulness, it also manifested itself in a complete avoidance of governmental power. He never even collaborated with it indirectly. He rejected Satan's offer (which the Bible more accurately terms a *temptation*) of control over all the kingdoms of the world.[15] When a crowd tried to thrust political power upon him by forcing him to be king, he fled to the mountains.[16] When the disciples asked Jesus who among them would be given the most power and prestige in his kingdom, he instructed them not to "lord" over others like the "rulers of the Gentiles" (Matt. 20:25). Maybe most importantly, when a Roman governor accused Jesus of leading an insurrection, Jesus declared that his kingdom and his followers do not employ such earthly power—they do not fight with violence.[17]

As I explore in more detail in Chapter 8 of *Jesus the Pacifist*, the eschewal of governmental power was a prominent theme throughout Jesus's ministry. At numerous points during his life, he could have directly employed governmental power, or indirectly partnered with it, to ostensibly further God's will, but he didn't. He advanced God's kingdom on earth by embodying, living, and speaking the kingdom, not by forcing it on others. He fought injustice through example, not control. He overcame evil by refusing to partake in its means, not by wielding its weapons more effectively or more justly. He refused to use political power to maintain social order, promote the common good, or ensure that history would turn out right. Instead, he humbly and patiently entrusted such things—the things we think we need to use government power for—to God, thereby bearing witness to his father's control over them. Despite all the material good he could seemingly have accomplished with governmental power, he shunned it.

Revelation calls God's followers to the same abstention. It never depicts Christians controlling or partnering with nations to advance God's kingdom and never instructs them to ensure—in any way, shape, or form—that government does its God-ordained job, upholds social morality, enforces social justice, or defends religious freedom. On the contrary, it portrays all earthly kings and kingdoms as God's enemies.

A voice from heaven declared, "Come out of [Babylon], my people, so that you will not share in her sins, so that you will not receive any of her plagues; for her sins are piled up to heaven, and God has remembered her crimes" (18:4-5). To "come out," as it is intended here, does not mean to physically leave earthly nations. It means to disassociate from their domineering, violence-driven way of life. Revelation instructs Christians not to revolt against government but to refuse to partake in its coercive rule. It also promises that those who receive the mark of the beast (which represents imperial power) will experience God's fury, while those who refuse it will be given authority over the nations and will reign with Jesus in eternity.[18]

When the Christian martyrs cried out to God for justice, "they were told to wait a little longer" (6:10-11). Like Jesus, they had dutifully entrusted judgment and vengeance to God, but unlike Jesus, they were becoming impatient. So God instructed them to keep trusting in his control and continue refraining from taking matters into their own hands. This is one of Revelation's main objectives: to convince Christians to remain faithful to the way of Jesus and leave vengeance to God, because *he* will execute it when the time is right (after all have ample opportunity to repent).

Revelation isn't unique in this regard. Throughout Scripture, God's followers are called to leave vengeance (and any violence it may entail) to him.[19] The admonition is found in every passage people cite to justify human violence, from the Old Testament to Romans 13 and all the way through Revelation. The Bible is crystal clear on this point: judgment and vengeance belong to God alone. Our task is simply to announce them (when appropriate, and in an appropriate manner), not to execute them. To do the latter is to usurp God's authority. Eventually, he will give us authority over the nations, but not yet.[20]

Resisting the allure of government's violence-based power and control has been a struggle for God's people since the beginning. "In the Bible there is really only one story: that of a people struggling to leave empire behind and set out to follow God," write Wes Howard-Brook and Anthony

Gwyther. "That story was to be relived whether in Egypt, Babylon, Rome, or elsewhere."[21] Indeed, God's followers seem stuck in a perpetual tug of war between turning to earthly kingdoms for their safety, comfort, and control and entrusting such things to him.

But if Revelation makes anything clear, it is that we advance God's kingdom on earth not by political means but by remaining faithful to the non-coercive way of Jesus. It doesn't call us to use earthly power to manage society, steer history, or ensure our own survival. It calls to bear witness to God's control of such things, which requires living as if we really believe in his control. We show we believe by not trying to control those things ourselves. Christians wage war by embodying Jesus's way of life, not by forcing it on others. We fight and conquer not by lording over others as empires do, but by selflessly serving others. We overcome violence by refusing to perpetuate it, by depriving its fire of oxygen, not by harnessing it for "good."

We can't have it both ways. We can't wield governmental power and advance God's kingdom on earth. The two are incompatible.

Governmental power is coercion-based. It relies on violence or the threat of it, which is why governments employ policemen and soldiers to impose fines, imprisonment, or death on those who disobey their edicts. Christ's power, on the other hand, is entirely nonviolent, relying on peaceful persuasion and exemplification instead, which is why the church employs preachers and servants instead of armed personnel.

As libertarian political philosophy has long pointed out, to employ government is to employ violence. If there's no need for the use or threat of physical force, then there's no need for government. Government is, by its very nature, physical force. Don't be fooled by the often veiled and indirect character of its force or the intentions of those wielding it. Whether wielded for personal gain or to help others, its violent nature remains. The "selfless" use of physical coercion is still the use of physical coercion.

This is why Revelation compares and contrasts God's kingdom with empire. They are precise opposites in both their means and their ends. One operates through violence, the other through nonviolence. One seeks its own safety and comfort at the expense of others, the other the safety and comfort of others at its own expense. One tries to conquer the world by dominating it, the other by loving it.

Hence the reason we must choose between using governmental power and advancing God's kingdom. To be entangled in the world's power struggles is to be engaged in trying to control Satan's kingdom, and as long as we are trying to manage Satan's kingdom, we are not advancing God's.

We cannot serve two masters. Only one can receive our full faith, trust, and allegiance. The Romans knew this, which is why faith in Caesar was considered a civic virtue and why a lack of such faith was considered atheism—a crime for which the earthly Christians were often indicted.

To put your trust and faith in government and its means of ruling is to cheat on God, which is why Revelation repeatedly refers to Babylon (a great city of wealth and power built upon violence) as a prostitute with whom the kings of the earth, and others, committed adultery.[22] She sold herself to another god—the god of imperial power—in exchange for a morsel of momentary pleasure, a smidgen of temporary control, and fleeting sense of safety. We make the same mistake when we climb into bed with governmental power.

This is also why Revelation describes the 144,000 as "those who did not defile themselves with women, for they remained virgins" (14:4). John isn't talking about literal sex. He is symbolically and metaphorically referring to remaining faithfully obedient to God instead of empire, which is why the very next sentence says, "They follow the Lamb wherever he goes."

Throughout the Bible, including in Revelation, prostitution and sexual infidelity are metaphors for idolatry.[23] Similarly, throughout the New Testament, the church is occasionally referred to as the bride of Christ, meaning it is betrothed to him and him alone.[24] Its duty is to remain faithful. And as we've just seen, that includes declining governmental power, for to employ such power is to ally with Satan's means of ruling.

For these reasons and others, the whole point of God's war against Satan is to eradicate earthly kingdoms and their modus operandi. He wants to replace Satan's way of ruling the world, as embodied in violence-driven governmental power, with his way of ruling the world, as embodied in the always-loving and wholly non-coercive slaughtered lamb. He sent Jesus to earth to become its sole king and to rule it with nonviolent love for all eternity, thereby banishing earthly governments to the dustbin of history. This is why Revelation repeatedly declares Jesus to be the world's rightful ruler, pits him against earthly kings, and ultimately depicts him triumphing over them.[25]

Notice that Jesus didn't redeem governmental power. He didn't restore it to its proper role, ensure that it was placed in the right hands, or otherwise harness it for good. He defeated it. "And having disarmed the powers and authorities, he made a public spectacle of them, triumphing over them by the cross" (Col. 2:15). His was a victory over violence itself, not merely its improper use.

Most importantly, Jesus achieved victory through love and for love. He fought and conquered through his testimony, by bearing witness to the truth in both word (symbolized by a sword coming out of his mouth) and deed (symbolized by a slaughtered lamb).

To summarize what Revelation demands of Christians, nothing in Revelation instructs or even implicitly encourages the use of violence, not now or ever. Precisely the opposite is the case. From every angle, whether literal or symbolic,

Revelation advocates faithfulness to Christlike nonviolence. There are a few debatable and difficult-to-understand aspects of Revelation, but this isn't one of them. The book of Revelation calls believers to the same nonviolent ethics that the rest of the New Testament requires, not to a more just or more effective type of violence.

Even if Revelation can be accurately read as depicting the use of actual violence by God, Jesus, or angels at the end of history, nothing about their future actions justifies human violence today. Everywhere and always in the New Testament, including in Revelation, we are called to obey and mimic the Jesus of the Gospels, not the God, Jesus, or angels of the violent parables or Revelation. Even if God plans to issue new instructions to use violence at some point in the future (and we have no reason to believe that he does), our current orders are to live and die like Jesus did—nonviolently.

Furthermore, even if we conclude that God, Jesus, or angels *do* use violence, their violence is always opposed to human violence. It is always employed to discourage and end human violence. Therefore, although Revelation's message about God's use or non-use of violence may not be as clear as we'd like, its message about human violence is clear: God hates human violence, and he will judge, punish, and eradicate it.

"The book often thought to overturn the ethic of nonviolence," concludes Sprinkle, "is actually its greatest defender."[26]

---

[1] This is what it means to proclaim the cross a victory, as we did in Chapter 2. The victory lies in remaining faithful unto death, in dying instead of compromising to survive.

[2] For verses that summarily advocate obedience to God, see 2:26 and 3:2-3, 8. For verses that summarily define God's people as those who obey him, see 12:17, 14:12, and 20:6. For verses that summarily warn us of judgment according to our deeds, see 2:23, 20:12-13, and 22:12.

3 To put it another way, although Revelation isn't a treatise on the ethics of violence, it definitely has something to say about the subject. It encourages us to remain faithful to what Jesus has already taught about it and looks forward to the eradication of violence, to a world without violence, to the kingdom of God.

4 John likely didn't even consider the possibility that using violent illustrations, in an effort to metaphorically communicate the reality of Jesus's war against and defeat of evil, could be interpreted as advocating for, or even endorsing, actual human violence. For John, Jesus's antiviolence was obvious and well-known.

5 Rev. 6:9-11; 7:13-15; 20:4-6; 22:14.

6 Rev. 13:10.

7 Rev. 1:17-18; 2:10; 11:1–13.

8 Rev. 1:9; 2:13; 7:13-15; 12:11; 17:6.

9 Of course, martyrdom isn't the goal. God doesn't want us to seek our own death for the sake of dying. The goal is faithful obedience, regardless of the cost. God calls us not to die but to be willing to die if necessary to avoid complicity with evil. Death is simply a *possible* byproduct of uncompromising faithfulness.

10 By "God's followers," I mean Christians generally. There is one instance (11:3-7) in which two unique, God-appointed witnesses are said to possess the ability to defend themselves with fire *from their mouths* and the power to unleash plagues. But they are never depicted doing so, and instead are martyred. N.T. Wright believes these two prophets are reminiscent of Moses and Elijah, each of whom stood up to oppression and idolatry by speaking the truth and calling forth plagues. "What John is saying," he contends, "is that the prophetic witness of the church, in the great tradition of Moses and Elijah, will perform powerful signs and thereby torment the surrounding unbelievers, but that the climax of their work will be their martyr-death …." See Kindle location 1777 in *Revelation for Everyone.*

11 Rev. 6:9-11; 7:14; 19:8, 14; 22:14.

12 Rev. 16:1-21; 17:16-17; 18:8, 20-21; 19:1-2, 11-21; 20:1-3, 7-10, 13-14.

13 Rev. 13:9-10; 14:12-13; 17:6; 18:24; 19:1-2.

14 Rev. 17:12-14; 19:14.

15 Luke 4:5-8.

16 John 6:1-15.

17 Luke 18:33-36.

18 Rev. 14:9-12; 16:2; 20:4.

19 Deut. 32:35; 1 Sam. 24:12-13; Isa. 30:18; 35:4; Prov. 20:22; Luke 6:37; 1 Pet. 2:19-23; Rom. 2:1-3; 12:19; 13:4; Heb. 10:30; 1 Cor. 5:12-13.

20 Rev. 2:26-27; 20:4.

21 Wes Howard-Brook and Anthony Gwyther, *Unveiling Empire: Reading Revelation Then and Now* (Orbis Books, 1999), 4727, Kindle.

22 Rev. 14:8; 17:2, 5-6; 18:3-4, 7, 9-20, 24; 19:1-8.

23 Exod. 34:15-16; Lev. 17:7; Num. 15:39; Deut. 31:16; Judg. 8:27; 1 Chron. 5:25; 2 Chron. 21:11; Isa. 1:21; 23:17; Jer. 2:20; 13:27; Ezek. 16:23-30; 23:7; Hosea 4:12; 5:4; Rev. 2:20-23; 14:8; 17:2, 4-5; 18:3, 9; 19:2.

24 Matt. 25:1-13; Mark 2:19-20; Luke 5:34-35; John 3:28-30; Rev. 18:23; 19:7; 21:2, 9; 22:17.

25 Rev. 1:4-5; 2:26-27; 3:14; 11:15; 12:5; 17:12-14; 19:15-16, 19-21.

26 Sprinkle, *Fight*, 2709.

CHAPTER 8

CONCLUSION

The key to reading Revelation nonviolently lies in respecting its literary genre by reading it symbolically, and then interpreting its symbols through the lens of the Gospels. Such an approach reveals its nonviolent themes. On the other hand, a genre-violating, literalistic, Gospel-disregarding interpretation completely misses the book's radical antiviolence message and instead causes the reader to walk away with a contradictory pro-violence impression.

Yes, John uses violent symbolism. But he also uses nonviolent symbolism. And he combines them in a way that subverts violence. He reveals violence to be Satan's means, not God's; powerless, not redemptive; beaten, not victorious. He exposes the myth of redemptive violence and unveils the truth of redemptive love.

Yes, Revelation's big-picture analogy describes warfare and violent conflict. Like the rest of the New Testament, it adopts the Old Testament's warfare worldview and continues its "holy war" tradition, both of which convey vital messages about God (e.g., that he despises and combats injustice). But also like the rest of the New Testament, Revelation redefines key elements of the Old Testament's perspective, particularly its view of violence. When John is told that the "Lion of the tribe of Judah" has triumphed, he hears the Old Testament's perspective on how to fight and conquer. But when he looks at the conqueror with his new Gospel glasses, he sees a slaughtered lamb and a new way of battling evil. Through such nuanced symbolism, John is telling us that the Old Testament's predictions of a conquering Messiah were correct, but its expectations for *how* he (and his followers) would conquer were not.

According to the entire New Testament, including Revelation, Jesus overcame violence and death, not by avoiding or controlling them, but by allowing them to do their worst to him—crucify him—and then rising from the dead, thereby demonstrating his power over them. He allowed himself to be "conquered" by violence and death so that he could show the world what real conquering looks like: uncompromising, self-sacrificial, nonviolent love—even unto death. Or, as John would say, it looks like lamb power, not lion power.

This is one of the mysteries unlocked by Jesus in the Gospels and symbolically highlighted in Revelation through Jesus's opening of the scroll. The most powerful force in the universe is Christlike love, not violence. But it took Jesus to reveal it. For the first time in recorded history, he associated self-sacrificial nonviolence with victory and success. Without him, the power of love would still be disguised as apparent weakness while the apparent power of violence would still be hiding its true weakness.

This is why the first sentence of John's book introduces itself as "the revelation from Jesus Christ." It is a report of what Jesus revealed—that God, not empire, is in control; that he, not Satan, has won, is winning, and will win; and that self-sacrificial love, not violence, conquers all. As Zahnd concludes, "The book of Revelation is not where the good news of the gospel goes to die" or "where the gospel becomes the anti-gospel" but "where the good news of the gospel finds its most creative expression."[1]

Not only is a nonviolent reading of Revelation possible, it is also responsible, rational, and scripturally based. It respects the book's historical and literary contexts, comports with the trajectory of the greater biblical narrative, confirms what the rest of the New Testament teaches, and, most importantly, is Christ-centered. Its conclusions arise from what came before it, the bigger picture within which it sits, and the axis around which it revolves—not from a few isolated, obscure, and ambiguous images. As a result, it is more theologically sound than any violent interpretation.

A symbolic, nonviolent reading of Revelation also produces better fruit than a literal, violent reading. After all, if Jesus will annihilate all non-Christians upon his return, what does it matter if we kill a few thousand here or there? And if God will eventually destroy the earth, why should we inconvenience ourselves with taking caring of it today?

So you have a choice. You can read Revelation violently or nonviolently. But why would you interpret it violently when there is an equally rational way to interpret it nonviolently? You don't even have to surrender your belief in God's wrath, judgment, or victory to do so.

---

[1] Zahnd, *Sinners in the Hands of a Loving God*, 2373.

AUTHOR'S NOTE

First, thank you for reading my book! I pray it has been a blessing.

Second, a little bit about me. I'm a reader, writer, and attorney with a passion for exploring God's beauty and brilliance. I live in Oklahoma City with my bride and our three children. If you'd like to learn more or sign up to be notified of future books and new blog posts, please visit my website at www.matthewcurtisfleischer.com. You can also find me on Facebook or on Twitter at @MatthewCurtisF.

Lastly, if you would like to help this book reach a wider audience, please consider (1) leaving a review on Amazon, Goodreads, or anywhere else readers visit and (2) mentioning it on social media. I'd be honored to have your help. Thank you!

Sincerely,
Matthew

MatthewCurtisFleischer@gmail.com

Special thanks to my bride Nicole, Pastor Aaron Bolerjack, and Dr. Marty Alan Michelson, each of whom generously made invaluable contributions to this book.